GROWING PAINS

BIBLE STUDY GUIDE

From the Bible-teaching ministry of

Charles R. Swindoll

INSIGHT FOR LIVING

Chuck graduated in 1963 from Dallas Theological Seminary, where he now serves as the school's fourth president, helping to prepare a new generation of men and women for the ministry. Chuck has served in pastorates in three states: Massachusetts, Texas, and California, including almost twenty-three years at the First Evangelical Free Church in Fullerton, California. He is currently senior pastor of Stonebriar Community Church in Frisco, Texas, north of Dallas. His sermon messages have been aired over radio since 1979 as the *Insight for Living* broadcast. A best-selling author, Chuck has written numerous books and booklets on many subjects.

Based on the outlines and transcripts of Chuck's sermons, the study guide text is co-authored by Lee Hough, a graduate of the University of Texas at Arlington and Dallas Theological Seminary.

Editor in Chief:
Cynthia Swindoll

Coauthor of text:
Lee Hough

Senior Study Guide Writer:
Jason Shepherd

Senior Editor and Assistant Writer:
Wendy Peterson

Copy Editors:
Karla Lenderink
Marco Salazar
Glenda Schlahta

Text Designer:
Gary Lett

Graphic System Administrator:
Bob Haskins

Director, Communications Division:
John Norton

Production Manager:
Don Bernstein

Printer:
Sinclair Printing Company

Unless otherwise identified, all Scripture references are from the New American Standard Bible, updated edition, copyright © The Lockman Foundation 1960, 1962, 1963, 1968, 1971, 1972, 1973, 1975, 1977, 1995. Used by permission. Scripture taken from the Holy Bible, New International Version © 1973, 1978, 1984 International Bible Society, used by permission of Zondervan Bible Publishers [NIV]. Other version cited is *The Message*.

An effort has been made to locate sources and obtain permission where necessary for the quotations used in this book. In the event of any unintentional omission, a modification will gladly be incorporated in future printings.

ISBN 1-57972-319-5
Study Guide Cover Design: Alex Pasieka
Cover Photograph: © Index Stock Imagery/1999
Printed in the United States of America

CONTENTS

1 Growing through Waiting 1
      Psalm 62:1–2

2 Growing through Failure 9
      Psalm 103

3 Growing through Misunderstanding 18
      Psalm 140

4 Growing through Loss 27
      Job 1–2

5 Growing through Mistakes 37
      Psalm 31

6 Growing through Weakness 44
      Psalm 46

7 Growing through Monotony 52
      Psalm 90

8 Growing through Fear 60
      Psalm 27

   Books for Probing Further 68

   Notes 71

   Ordering Information 75

INTRODUCTION

You've no doubt heard the old cliché

No Pain, No Gain.

It's an old saying, but it's still true! Nobody ever escapes pain in the process of growth—not even Christians. Especially not Christians. We simply *cannot* become the people God meant us to be without some headaches and heartaches. Even Jesus our Lord "learned obedience from the things which He suffered" (Heb. 5:8).

This eight-chapter study is a realistic series of biblical messages about life in God's family—a life that includes disappointments, mistakes, struggles, hardships, and misunderstandings. Not a moment, however, is spent apart from God's watchful eye. Hopefully, each chapter will bring you reassurance and renewed determination to trust God and hang tough.

The road from earth to heaven is not an easy, downhill slide. It is, rather, a challenge that forces us to look to Him who has gone before us. He *will* see us through! Each tough experience simply reminds us that we are on the right road.

Chuck Swindoll

PUTTING TRUTH
INTO ACTION

K nowledge apart from application falls short of God's desire for His children. He wants us to apply what we learn so that we will change and grow. This study guide was prepared with these goals in mind. As you go through the following pages, we hope your desire to discover biblical truth will grow as your understanding of God's Word increases and that you will be encouraged to apply what you've learned.

To assist you in your study, we've included a section called ❀ Living Insights at the end of each lesson. These exercises will challenge you to study further and to think of specific ways to put your discoveries into action.

On occasion a lesson is followed by a ⬥ Digging Deeper section, which gives you additional information and resources to probe further into some issues raised in that lesson.

There are many ways to use this guide—in personal devotions, group studies, discussions with friends and family, and Sunday school classes. And, of course, it's an ideal study aid when you're listening to its corresponding *Insight for Living* radio series.

To benefit most from this study guide, we would encourage you to consider it a spiritual journal. That's why we've included space in the **Living Insights** for recording your thoughts and discoveries. We hope you'll return to those sections often for review and encouragement as you continue to grow in your walk with Christ.

Lee M. Hough

Lee Hough
Coauthor of Text

GROWING
PAINS

Chapter 1

GROWING THROUGH WAITING

Psalm 62

Waiting.

Isn't that just your favorite thing to do? What could be more fun than a slow line at the bank? Or a long, long, long train making you late for work? Or an eternity of dull magazines at the doctor's office?

None of us likes to wait. We get frustrated and impatient, frazzled and worn out. And when the wait involves something serious, like having a home in escrow, hearing back after a job interview, or getting biopsy results, we can struggle with fear and discouragement and anxiety and anger.

Waiting is never easy, but it's a part of life we cannot escape—no matter how hard we try. This is especially true for Christians. We are called to order our lives around God's purposes and plans, and that means waiting on His timing rather than our own. His way of doing things, not ours, is to become our priority. Consider, for example, the men and women in the Bible whom God called to do His will. Every single one of them had to endure a time of waiting, and it was often painful.

- **Noah.** During the years he built the ark, Noah most likely endured his neighbors' derision and perhaps his own doubts. Remember, it had never rained before. And once he was inside the ark, it was more than a year before he stepped on dry land again.

- **Job.** His life's work wiped out in an instant, his children killed with one calamitous stroke, his health ravaged—Job struggled to find God's reason for his anguish. Waiting was no serene exercise for him; he railed at the incompetent and insensitive counsel of his friends and raged at God's seeming unfairness, until he was humbled by God's own words in the midst of the storm.

1

- **Abraham and Sarah.** *Barren.* The word hounded Sarah for eighty-nine years. Finally, when she was ninety and Abraham was one hundred, they had their first child together, Isaac, the child of God's promise—a promise that God had declared to Abraham twenty-five years before.

- **Joseph.** He endured years in an Egyptian prison for a crime he didn't commit. But rather than withering and dying, Joseph's faith grew through the wait because he trusted in God's sovereignty.

- **Moses.** Because he ran ahead of God's timing and took justice in his own hands, Moses spent forty years in the obscurity of the Midian desert. Here he learned that you either go with God or you don't go at all. It would also take the Hebrews, Moses' people, another forty years to learn to trust God's ways instead of their own.

- **The Prophets.** From Elijah to Malachi, the prophets all announced God's words to His people and waited for them to return to Him. Sometimes the people repented, but more often than not, they ignored the prophets' warnings and went their own destructive way.

- **Paul.** After a humbling encounter with the risen Christ, Paul—temporarily blinded—waited three days before his sight was restored. The rest of his life was spent waiting on God to direct his steps, sharing the gospel wherever God would lead him.

One thing's for sure—we're not alone in having to wait. But is there anything that can help make waiting more endurable? More productive even, so that our character grows toward God rather than away from Him in despair? Let's turn to the Scriptures to see what help the Lord has provided.

Initial Observations about Waiting

From our roster of the Bible's "waiters," we can draw out two truths about waiting.

First, *waiting on God is the rule rather than the exception.* All of us have a natural tendency to make waiting on God the *exception* and trusting in our own wisdom and strength the *rule.* When there are no open doors, we try to force the locks. But God's provisions don't always come along the minute we want them to. And we may not know His purposes until we get to heaven. We must learn to accept that, in many areas of our lives, waiting will be the very process God uses to mature us.

Second, *waiting on God means resting, not worrying.* It's a matter of trust, isn't it? As David wrote in Psalm 31,

> But as for me, I trust in You, O Lord,
> I say, "You are my God."
> My times are in Your hand. (vv. 14–15a)

All our times are in His hands, even the slow waits. But resting doesn't mean being passive, inert. Waiting is active—think of Noah hammering together the ark; think of Joseph being put in charge of the other prisoners because the Lord was with him. Life goes on, God is with us, and we need to be present and involved—whatever our situation. So stay active while you wait, just don't be anxious.

Let's turn to another of David's psalms and learn a few pointers on how to wait productively.

Waiting in Tough Times

Waiting on the Lord is hardest when we're in a pinch. David was certainly no stranger to tough times. During one crisis, he transposed his faith into a song, Psalm 62, that gives encouragement to other "waiters."

What to Do

We first learn from David's words to *focus on God.*

> My soul waits in silence for God only . . .
> My soul, wait in silence for God only. (vv. 1a, 5a)

"For God only" we are to wait, David reiterates. Not panicking over our circumstances, not fretting over the meanness of other people who are doing us wrong. And David had his enemies.

> How long will you assail a man,
> That you may murder him, all of you,
> Like a leaning wall, like a tottering fence?
> They have counseled only to thrust him down
>   from his high position;
> They delight in falsehood;
> They bless with their mouth,
> But inwardly they curse. (vv. 3–4)

David found rest, though, in God, who is always in control and who always cares for us. The infinite God is certainly greater than any temporal enemy or passing trouble.

Second, David's words remind us to *trust in God's character*. We find our rest in focusing on God because we know His character is holy and absolutely dependable.

> From Him is my salvation.
> He only is my rock and my salvation,
> My stronghold; I shall not be greatly shaken. . . .
> For my hope is from Him.
> He only is my rock and my salvation,
> My stronghold; I shall not be shaken.
> On God my salvation and my glory rest;
> The rock of my strength, my refuge is in God.
> Trust in Him at all times, O people;
> Pour out your heart before Him;
> God is a refuge for us. . . .
> Once God has spoken;
> Twice I have heard this:
> That power belongs to God;
> And lovingkindness is Yours, O Lord.
> (vv. 1b–2, 5b–8, 11–12a)

What does David mean when he calls God his "rock"? The Hebrew word for *rock*, *tsur*, conveys the idea that God "is totally reliable. He is a sure source of strength and he endures throughout every generation."[1] Not only is He steadfast, but He is a stronghold of safety, a shelter of protection, the One who delivers us and gives us hope. He is all-powerful and loving beyond our power to comprehend.

Who better to provide for our needs during the tough times of waiting? People who rely on God as their Rock will not be moved.

How to Wait

From David, we can also learn two ways to practice waiting. The first way is *in silence*. The Hebrew word for *silence* in verse 1 is *dumiyyah*, meaning "a quiet waiting, repose." It pictures rest. In

---

1. *Theological Wordbook of the Old Testament*, ed. R. Laird Harris, Gleason L. Archer Jr., Bruce K. Waltke (Chicago, Ill.: Moody Press, 1980), vol. 2, p. 762.

verse 5, the Hebrew word is *damam*, "to be or grow dumb, silent or still." With our mouths and hearts stilled, we can meditate on the things of the Lord. During these times of quietness God may bring to mind a needed truth, a praise, something to be thankful for, or a practical application of His Word that we had been missing.

The second way is *in confidence*. "I shall not be greatly shaken," David says in verse 2; then again in verse 6, "I shall not be shaken." Why? Because of God's character and His provision. We can wait secure and stable in His love. He saves, shelters, and strengthens us. The prophet Isaiah explained that God even exchanges our weakness for His strength when we wait on Him.

> Yet those who wait for the Lord
> Will gain new strength;
> They will mount up with wings like eagles,
> They will run and not get tired,
> They will walk and not become weary. (Isa. 40:31)

No wonder David urges us to trust in God "at all times" (Ps. 62:8)!

Why Wait?

Why should we wait on God and do things His way? David provides part of the answer for us in verses 9–10:

> Men of low degree are only vanity and men of
>   rank are a lie;
> In the balances they go up;
> They are together lighter than breath.
> Do not trust in oppression
> And do not vainly hope in robbery;
> If riches increase, do not set your heart upon
>   them.

Compared with the infinite God, humanity can't even budge the scale. We humans are transitory; the power and wealth we strive for is fleeting. And it may look like we got away with harming others to get what we wanted, but as David reminds us, the Lord "recompense[s] a man according to his work" (v. 12b). How much better it is to wait for that which has substance and eternal worth than grab for the quick, empty comforts.

Waiting for God results in priceless benefits. They include:

- deliverance: "From Him is my salvation" (v. 1b)

5

- security: "He only is my rock . . . my stronghold" (vv. 2, 6)
- hope: "For my hope is from Him" (v. 5b)
- glory: "On God my salvation and my glory rest" (v. 7a)
- refuge: "My refuge is in God" (v. 7b; see also v. 8)

Practical Application for Today

A student once asked the president of his school if there was a course he could take that was shorter than the one prescribed. "Oh yes," answered the president, "but then it depends upon what you want to be. When God wants to make an oak, He takes a hundred years, but when He wants to make a squash, He takes six months."[2]

Many of us, while waiting on God, have asked a similar question, "Lord, isn't there a shorter, less difficult route I could take?" But it's only by waiting on Him that our roots will grow deep enough for us to be as solid as an oak.

Three truths emerge from this study on waiting that are well worth reflecting on:

1. Waiting involves trusting.

2. Waiting includes praying.

3. Waiting implies resting.

It may not be our favorite thing to do, but waiting is one of God's most effective methods for growing us into patient, wise, humble, and mature Christians.

🌸 *Living Insights*

Margaret Thatcher, former prime minister of Great Britain, once remarked, "I am extraordinarily patient provided I get my own way in the end."[3]

---

2. Miles J. Stanford, *Principles of Spiritual Growth* (Lincoln, Neb.: Back to the Bible, 1977), p. 12.

3. Margaret Thatcher, as quoted in *Observer* (London, January 2, 1983), from *The Columbia Dictionary of Quotations*, licensed from Columbia University Press, © 1993 by Columbia University Press. All rights reserved. From Microsoft Bookshelf © 1987–1995 Microsoft Corporation. All rights reserved.

Isn't that the truth for most of us! And isn't the uncertainty of how things will turn out at the heart of why waiting is so hard? Let's take some time to examine our hearts in light of what we've studied in our chapter. It may not make waiting go any quicker, but it may help us become more patient and peaceful throughout the process.

Are you in a time of waiting right now? What is your situation? How have you been coping with it so far?

_____

_____

_____

_____

_____

Have you been able to trust God through the wait? Or has this experience begun to shake your confidence in Him, in His love and His promises?

_____

_____

_____

_____

_____

Have you talked to Him about it? Have you taken your fears and disappointments to God in prayer? Or have you withdrawn? Have you been afraid to tell Him what you feel? What would you like to say to Him?

_____

_____

_____

_____

One thing about God, He's never taken by surprise—not by how we feel, what we're thinking, or what we'd like to say. And another thing, He always loves us. As David said in another of his psalms (which we'll explore in more depth in our next chapter),

> Just as a father has compassion on his children,
> So the Lord has compassion on those who fear
> Him.
> For He Himself knows our frame;
> He is mindful that we are but dust.
> (Ps. 103:13–14)

Perhaps you need to remind yourself of God's character and how trustworthy He is. Take some time to read through Psalm 145. What stands out to you? What flies directly to your heart? Do any other Scriptures come to mind? Jot them down.

_____

_____

_____

_____

_____

God may end your waiting tomorrow . . . or He may not. But He is with you; He goes before you; He comes behind you (Matt. 28:20; Isa. 52:12). He desires your good even more than you desire it. So rest in Him. Are you trying to do things your own way, in your own strength and wisdom? Ask the Lord to reveal any hurtful ways in you. Then write them down, and let them go. And rest in the Lord who loves you.

_____

_____

_____

Chapter 2

GROWING THROUGH FAILURE

Psalm 103

How many of us got one of these in school? An "F." A failing grade. A test handed back to us facedown, if the teacher was merciful. A paper we carefully folded and hid in our pocket, safe from the jeers of other students and from the disapproving looks of our parents. That "F" felt like a scarlet letter, a brand that seared us with shame and marked not just our work but us as failures.

Well, if you've lived very long, you know that an "F" in school is barely remembered after you've floundered and failed for awhile in life. From diets we just can't seem to stay on to enslaving addictions we can't seem to break. From friendships we've damaged to marriages we've let crumble before our eyes. From job interviews we've fumbled to businesses we've lost. And how about those heartbreaking spiritual failures, when we've had to face the same sins, the same doubts, the same breaking points over and over and over again?

God must be disgusted with us, right? "Here comes Sam—again," we imagine God saying, "Isn't that clod ever going to get it right?"

Nothing could be further from God's heart.

"My thoughts are not your thoughts," God tells us. "My ways are higher than your ways," and His ways involve compassion and abundant pardon (Isa. 55:7–9). He is a God of second and third and fourth and fifth chances—and even more. His hands are extended to help, and His words are given to encourage us to grow.

Initial Facts about Failure

We're often taken by surprise by our failures, but really, they are a natural part of life. A painful part, but normal nevertheless because we are human—which means imperfect, fallible, messy. God knows and expects this. But the trouble comes when others can't accept this truth about us, or we can't accept it about ourselves. Pressures from these two areas only intensify the pain of failure.

Two Real Pressures That Intensify Our Pain

Our first pressure comes from *other people*. When we fail, we will invariably get more flack from other people—including fellow Christians—than we ever will from God. Who of us hasn't been kicked when we were down? Who hasn't been harshly blamed rather than gently restored? People will often discourage us, but God's ways, remember, are more merciful than that.

Our second pressure comes from *ourselves*. That's right, sometimes other people aren't the problem. Sometimes we're our own worst judge and jury, only too ready to pronounce a guilty verdict. Many of us stagger under self-imposed loads of guilt, worthlessness, disqualification, and condemnation. We refuse to forgive ourselves, deciding that we can never change and robbing ourselves of hope. We give up on ourselves when God is just rolling up His sleeves to begin the work of renewing and restoring.

One Major Problem That Perpetuates Defeat

Why do we keep beating up and giving up on ourselves? One major reason is *a preoccupation with unrealistic standards*. Somewhere along the line we got the idea that we are supposed to be super-Christians: maturing faster than a speeding sermon series, more powerful than a trainload of temptations, able to leap human imperfection in a single bound. But instead of an "S" emblazoned across our chests, we wind up sewing a sorry "F" on a rumpled costume we can't quite fill out.

Here's the truth, though: We're not going to save the whole world for Christ; no one person can do that. We're not going to live a sinless life; only Christ did that. We're not going to make perfect decisions; only God is all-seeing, all-knowing, all-wise, and all-loving. We're just normal, garden-variety human beings in need of God's redemption and constant care. And that's not only OK—it's biblical! We are "earthen vessels," as Paul calls us (2 Cor. 4:7), or "cracked pots," as Patsy Clairmont paraphrases![1] And cracked

---

1. "Picture an empty pitcher with a network of cracks down the front," writes Patsy Clairmont. "Now imagine that pitcher filled with light and a lid put on the top. Where does the light shine through? The cracks. That is the same way the Lord's light shines through our lives." A bit of encouragement, at no extra charge, from her book *God Uses Cracked Pots* (Colorado Springs, Colo.: Focus on the Family Publishing, 1991), p. 1.

pots will leak and spill, but once they've been in the hands of the Mender, they can again hold beauty for all to see.

Five Practical Ways to Recover from Failure

In Psalm 103, David turns to the Mender of our lives with thanksgiving and praise. As we learn five practical ways to recover from failure, let's imbibe David's spirit of hope in God's vast goodness to refresh our weary hearts and help us get back on our feet.

Responsibility: You're Accountable for Your Reaction

How we respond to our failures is our responsibility. And that, by the way, includes taking responsibility for our part in them. If we blame others and never face what we have done through our choices and actions, we keep God at arm's length, not allowing Him to work within us.

But if we attack ourselves with blame, or if we stew in anger, surrender to discouragement, or allow our spirits to sour in bitterness, we haven't helped matters much either. Because we've taken our eyes off God, the greatness of His character, and the limitless scope of His power—power that He wants to use on our behalf. Look at what David wrote:

> Bless the Lord, O my soul,
> And all that is within me, bless His holy name.
> Bless the Lord, O my soul,
> And forget none of His benefits. (Ps. 103:1–2)

Bless the Lord—be thankful—in the midst of failure? That's right. Erwin W. Lutzer, in his book *Failure: The Back Door to Success*, explains this for us.

> Thanksgiving is a sign of trust; if we believe that all things work together for good, we will be able to be thankful in the most depressing circumstances. Paul's advice is basic to our victory: "In everything give thanks; for this is God's will for you in Christ Jesus" (1 Thessalonians 5:18).
>
> Even if you don't *feel* particularly thankful, thank God for your blessings in Christ (e.g., forgiveness, acceptance, and righteousness), and your attitude will change. I've found that the most difficult struggle is to begin to consciously thank God for all

things; then when I think of all God's blessings, my second difficulty is to know when to quit.[2]

David would have us "forget none of His benefits"—good counsel that provides us with another practical way to recover from failure.

Focus: Replace Blaming with Claiming God's Grace

Just consider all the benefits God has given us:

> Who pardons all your iniquities,
> Who heals all your diseases;
> Who redeems your life from the pit,
> Who crowns you with lovingkindness and
>   compassion;
> Who satisfies your years with good things,
> So that your youth is renewed like the eagle.
> The Lord performs righteous deeds
> And judgments for all who are oppressed.
> He made known His ways to Moses,
> His acts to the sons of Israel.
> The Lord is compassionate and gracious,
> Slow to anger and abounding in
>   lovingkindness. . . .
> He has not dealt with us according to our sins,
> Nor rewarded us according to our iniquities.
> For as high as the heavens are above the earth,
> So great is His lovingkindness toward those who
>   fear Him.
> As far as the east is from the west,
> So far has He removed our transgressions from us.
> (vv. 3–8, 10–12)

Wow! He *pardons*—forgives—even our failures and all that led to them. He *heals* us. He *redeems*, or delivers, us from the pit we've fallen into. He *crowns* us with love, kindness, and compassion. He *satisfies* us with good things all through our lives. And he *renews* our strength—He lifts us up and helps us soar again. Oh, gracious and merciful God, so much bigger than our problems and limitations!

Do you also see that He doesn't gauge His love on conditions? "He has not dealt with us according to our sins, Nor rewarded us

2. Erwin W. Lutzer, *Failure: The Back Door to Success* (Chicago, Ill.: Moody Press, 1975), pp. 135–36.

according to our iniquities," David reminds us (v. 10). We may believe that God will be happy with us only if we read our Bible every day or pray and tithe regularly—and that if we don't, God frowns on us with displeasure. But that's a lie from the devil. That's turning God's grace into our works.

The truth is, God is the One to whom we can *always* turn, warts and all. We can bring Him the crushing, crumbling experiences of failure, and He will never shame us. We can come to Him again and again, at any time of day or night, and He'll never treat us as an annoying interruption. Instead, we'll hear Him say, "Here is My love. Here is My compassion." That's grace we can rest secure in.

Security: Count on God's Constant Acceptance and Understanding

David's next words further anchor us in God's compassion:

> Just as a father has compassion on his children,
> So the Lord has compassion on those who fear
>   Him.
> For He Himself knows our frame;
> He is mindful that we are but dust. (vv. 13–14)

From dust we were formed, and to dust we will one day return (Gen. 3:19). That doesn't mean we're as worthless as dirt! It's another way of saying that we are finite, that we are "but flesh, a passing breeze that does not return" (Ps. 78:39 NIV). Yet how we strive to achieve great, lasting things in order to prove our worth to ourselves and others.

Much of our discouragement when we fail comes when our human frailty is not taken into account. It also comes from taking our security from the performance-based acceptance of others. God, however, understands our limitations. He already knows our hearts, our motives, our worst failings. And He still reaches out to us with the compassion of a faithful father when we return to Him (see the parable of the father of the prodigal son in Luke 15).

Perspective: Refuse to Compare Yourself with Others, and Keep Your Eyes on the Lord

Why do we worry so much about what others think, about how we stack up next to them? David gives us some much-need perspective:

> As for man, his days are like grass;

As a flower of the field, so he flourishes.
When the wind has passed over it, it is no more,
And its place acknowledges it no longer.
(Ps. 103:15–16)

In the big, eternal picture, people are here and gone in the blink of an eye. Like a little flower whose beauty blooms for a few days and whose petals are scattered on the wind soon after, so are we. And so are the standards by which we measure ourselves against each other. We don't need to look at the person who has never lost a job, or who is a younger, yet more mature Christian than we are. Instead, we need to keep our eyes on the One who is here forever.

But the lovingkindness of the Lord is from everlasting to everlasting on those who fear Him,
And His righteousness to children's children. (v. 17)

If we grade ourselves on human opinion, we may never get up after a failure. But if we count on the Lord's everlasting love and righteousness, we can put our failure in perspective and gain the courage to go on.

Morale: Continue to Obey the Lord

Have you ever failed so badly that you felt like giving up on the Christian life? Like stomping away from God and slamming the door after you? At times like those, we need to check our spirits and remember who we're dealing with.

The Lord has established His throne in the
heavens,
And His sovereignty rules over all.
Bless the Lord, you His angels,
Mighty in strength, who perform His word,
Obeying the voice of His word!
Bless the Lord, all you His hosts,
You who serve Him, doing His will.
Bless the Lord, all you works of His,
In all places of His dominion;
Bless the Lord, O my soul! (vv. 19–22)

In our despair, Satan will tempt us to curse God. But we mustn't let him! The Lord is blessed above all—we really cannot compre-hend His greatness. "As the heavens are higher than the earth,"

14

remember, so are His ways and thoughts higher than ours (Isa. 55:9). The mighty angels obey His word, and their testimony encourages us to humbly continue to serve the Lord, to do His will, to obey Him, and to stand firm in His love and compassion. He is sovereign and knows what He is doing. Let's hang onto that truth when our morale threatens to cave in.

Some Final Thoughts

With God's abundant grace and help available to us, no one needs to live under the shadow of a giant "F." We're not marked for failure but for love. So control your expectations of yourself—don't set your standards unrealistically high, but leave room to be human. And leave the results with God.

Remember, from the world's point of view, Jesus Christ looked like a failure. He was born in a stable, of all places. He never amassed any wealth. His career was cut short by a clash with the authorities. But from God's perspective, He succeeded in securing something more precious than anyone could realize—our eternal salvation.

What may appear like a failure from our limited viewpoint may in fact be God's way of bringing about something good. But we must choose whether to give up or grow up through the experience. Which will it be for you?

Living Insights

The following notice was spotted in a small-town barbecue restaurant:

> REWARD: Lost dog. Three legs, blind in left eye, right ear missing, tail broken, recently neutered. Answers to the name "Lucky."

"Lucky"? Seems like he ought to be named "Poor Baby"! If it's true that we can grow from our mistakes and failures, old Lucky must have been either a mighty smart dog or a real slow learner.

Has life knocked you around a bit too? Has failure put a limp in your walk and a crimp in your tail? Do you wonder if you'll ever learn? Don't give up. Rather, take some time to apply the lessons you've learned in this chapter. Examine your approach to failure in light of the following questions, and ask the Lord to show you where you most need to grow.

Have you taken responsibility for your reactions? Why or why not? Is it difficult to do? Explain your situation.

_____

_____

_____

It's easy to blame others or yourself for failure. It boils down to a matter of focus. On what or whom are you focusing your failure? Why?

_____

_____

_____

Why is it important to be assured of God's complete acceptance? Do you feel you have to perform in order to be acceptable to God? Feel free to bring in Scriptures that touch on this subject.

_____

_____

_____

How do you decide if you've failed—by looking at yourself, at others, or at God? What are the obvious dangers of comparing yourself with others? What are the subtle dangers?

_____

_____

_____

How can failure be used to deepen your commitment to God? How has God used failure in your past to do that very work?

_____

_____

_____

_____

Proverbs 24:16 tells us that "a righteous man falls seven times, and rises again." With God's help, we can get back on our feet after failure has knocked us flat. Spend some time in prayer now, especially focusing on God's compassion. Ask Him to help you not give up but grow up to be the person He wants you to be.

Chapter 3

GROWING THROUGH MISUNDERSTANDING

Psalm 140

Few things in life can wound our relationships more than misunderstandings. The lesions they form are often painfully difficult to heal—if they can be healed at all.

Misunderstandings can occur between people who are hundreds of miles apart or just inches from each other. Letters, phone calls, e-mails, speeches, sermons, sometimes even our silences—all are potential carriers of this blight that affects our relationships. In his book *Communication: Key to Your Marriage*, Norman Wright gives us insight into why misunderstandings develop so easily.

> When you stop to think about all that's involved in getting your message across it's apparent why misunderstandings often occur. Communication specialists point out that when you talk with another person there are actually six messages that can come through.
> 1. What you mean to say.
> 2. What you actually say.
> 3. What the other person hears.
> 4. What the other person thinks he hears.
> 5. What the other person says about what you said.
> 6. What you think the other person said about what you said.[1]

It's a wonder we can communicate accurately at all! In fact, sometimes doesn't it feel like we're saying something like this: "I know you believe you understand what you think I said, but I'm not sure you realize that what you heard is not what I meant"[2]?

Have you ever misunderstood someone else, misread that person's motives? Or have you been on the receiving end of such

1. H. Norman Wright, *Communication: Key to Your Marriage* (Glendale, Calif.: Gospel Light Publications, 1974), p. 54.

2. Wright, *Communication: Key to Your Marriage*, p. 53.

treatment? Are you in the midst of a misunderstanding right now? Take courage. You *can* learn how to grow through this painful time. And God's Word can help.

Some Background about Misunderstanding

To start, let's look at the general cause of misunderstanding and then specifically at David's experience with it.

In Our Case

Every misunderstanding develops essentially the same way. First, an innocent act, word, or motive is misinterpreted by someone who—based on this faulty perception—then becomes offended at the innocent person.

In David's Case

David knew this all too well. After killing the giant Goliath, he ran headlong into a gigantic misunderstanding with King Saul. When the king and his warriors returned from conquering the Philistines, who had fled when David slew Goliath, they were met by an entourage of ecstatic women singing their praises.

> It happened as they were coming, when David returned from killing the Philistine, that the women came out of all the cities of Israel, singing and danc-ing, to meet King Saul, with tambourines, with joy and with musical instruments. The women sang as they played, and said,
> "Saul has slain his thousands,
> And David his ten thousands."
> (1 Sam. 18:6–7)

When Saul heard the song, jealousy set in—as well as a para-noia that twisted his perception of David as a good man into that of a power-hungry usurper.

> Then Saul became very angry, for this saying dis-pleased him; and he said, "They have ascribed to David ten thousands, but to me they have ascribed thousands. Now what more can he have but the kingdom?" Saul looked at David with suspicion from that day on. (vv. 8–9)

19

Though God had told the prophet Samuel to privately anoint David to be the next king (16:1–13), David was in no way scheming to take the throne away from Saul. By facing Goliath, he had only wanted to stand up for God's honor. In fact, the king would never have a more devoted servant than David. And yet, because of Saul's own insecurities and lack of faith, Israel's great victory became a rupture in the king's relationship with the young warrior—a wound that would fester until Saul's death.

The Misery of Misunderstanding

A number of Old Testament scholars believe that David's lament in Psalm 140 arose from his long struggle with the king who misread his motives.[3] Saul knew that God had left him and was with David, which made him afraid (1 Sam. 18:12). Rather than repenting and returning to God, the king chose to persecute the Lord's anointed. He turned away from God and toward evil, and as James Montgomery Boice reminds us, "Evil people hate those who are being saved by God and often try to destroy them."[4]

If you've ever had a misunderstanding turn into mistrust, and had that mistrust turn into hatred, then Psalm 140 is for you. David articulates so well this painful experience, capturing his own vulnerability and apprehension as well as Saul's escalating imaginings and relentless persecution.

Vulnerability

David's words to the Lord show that he feels highly exposed: "Rescue me, O Lord, . . . Preserve me" (Ps. 140:1), "Keep me, O Lord, . . . Preserve me" (v. 4).

We cannot protect ourselves from being misunderstood and misjudged, which leaves us feeling defenseless and vulnerable. Sometimes we cannot stop a misunderstanding once it has begun. And

---

3. See Joseph Addison Alexander, *The Psalms: Translated and Explained* (1873; reprint, Grand Rapids, Mich.: Baker Book House, 1977), pp. 542–43; Matthew Henry, *Commentary on the Whole Bible*, one-volume edition (Grand Rapids, Mich.: Zondervan Publishing House, Regency Reference Library, 1961), p. 725. Some commentators link Psalms 140 through 144 as a unit and see in Psalm 142's superscription—"Maskil of David, when he was in the cave"—a reference to David's hiding from Saul in the cave of Adullam (see 1 Sam. 22:1). This would set all these psalms, then, in the time of Saul's persecution of David.

4. James Montgomery Boice, *Psalms, Volume 3: Psalms 107–150* (Grand Rapids, Mich.: Baker Books, 1998), p. 1218.

though our instincts tell us to defend ourselves, this can make things worse. David experienced the painful reality that he was completely helpless to change the opinion of the one who had taken offense at him and who was retaliating against him for imagined wrongs.

Escalation

If slight misunderstandings rarely stay that way, think of what happened to Saul's gross misreading of David's character. Saul's distortion of the truth billowed up into an ominous storm front of cruelty and evil.

> Rescue me, O Lord, from evil men;
> Preserve me from violent men
> Who devise evil things in their hearts;
> They continually stir up wars. (vv. 1–2)

When people start with a misunderstanding, sadly, they don't always stop there. They often add to it, allowing escalating fantasies to run a dark course. In Saul's case, he became violent—twice he tried to pin David to the wall with his spear (1 Sam. 18:10–11; 19:9–10). From then on, he was bent on killing David.

Apprehension

Understandably, David felt apprehensive. Not only was Saul out to get him, he was undoubtedly trying to turn others against David with stinging slander and corrosive lies.

> They sharpen their tongues as a serpent;
> Poison of a viper is under their lips. (Ps. 140:3)

Persecution

With violent, slanderous Saul and his army hunting him like an animal, David found his best help in the Lord. Only God could keep him free from his enemies' entangling traps and safe from a deadly fall.

> Keep me, O Lord, from the hands of the wicked;
> Preserve me from violent men
> Who have purposed to trip up my feet.
> The proud have hidden a trap for me, and cords;
> They have spread a net by the wayside;
> They have set snares for me. (vv. 4–5)

Probably very few of us have had a misunderstanding turn deadly. Many of us, though, have most likely lost a friend, or even had a friend become an enemy, through a misreading of meaning and motives. How can we move through the misery to find good in life again?

Growth during Misunderstanding

Even through his pain, David held onto his faith in the Lord. It's so easy for us to let go of our faith and blame God for the meanness of others, for the hard and unfair situations we must live with. But we need to remember that faith is usually "developed through hardship, disappointment, disillusionment, conflict, frustration, failure, loss—not through stained glass nor sweet religious props."[5]

We will grow the most when we live out our church-nurtured faith in a world that inevitably misunderstands us. Life is not a fairy tale where doing the right thing automatically results in a happy outcome. Just think of David.

What can we learn from him? Three lessons.

First, David opens the door for growth by declaring his allegiance to the Lord. Rather than surrendering to his enemies or to despair, he entrusts himself to the One who understands, who sees the truth and judges fairly.

> I said to the Lord, "You are my God;
> Give ear, O Lord, to the voice of my supplica-
> tions." (v. 6)

Next, he reminds himself of the Lord's protection, counting on Him for his defense. Rather than retaliating against his enemies in his own strength, David seeks the refuge of God as his shield.

> "O God the Lord, the strength of my salvation,
> You have covered my head in the day of battle."
> (v. 7)

Finally, David asks the Lord to thwart the desires and devices of Saul and his army. In short, he asks the Lord to "boomerang on the heads of the wicked what they have spoken" and planned against him.[6]

---

5. Pamela Reeve, *Faith Is* . . . (Sisters, Ore.: Multnomah Books, 1994), n.p.

6. Willem A. VanGemeren, "Psalms," in *The Expositor's Bible Commentary*, gen. ed. Frank E. Gaebelein (Grand Rapids, Mich.: Zondervan Publishing House, 1991), vol. 5, p. 843.

"Do not grant, O Lord, the desires of the wicked;
Do not promote his evil device, that they not be
    exalted.
As for the head of those who surround me,
May the mischief of their lips cover them.
May burning coals fall upon them;
May they be cast into the fire,
Into deep pits from which they cannot rise.
May a slanderer not be established in the earth;
May evil hunt the violent man speedily."
(vv. 8–11)

The Assurance after Misunderstanding

As David concludes his psalm, we see his grasp on the divine perspective.

I know that the Lord will maintain the cause of
    the afflicted
And justice for the poor.
Surely the righteous will give thanks to Your
    name;
The upright will dwell in Your presence.
(vv. 12–13)

David sees that God will uphold the cause of all those who are suffering injustice. We need never feel abandoned, even during those times when the whole world seems to be set on fire against us by a tongue fueled with misunderstanding.

That sense of God's support should inspire tremendous gratefulness . . . not only *after* our affliction, but *during* it as well. By transferring our burdens to the Lord, we can know the fullness of joy that comes from dwelling in His presence (see Ps. 16:11).

❧ *Living Insights*

As we grow in the Lord, all of us will encounter misunderstandings. Like David, when he slew Goliath, some of our greatest words and deeds done in pure faith will be attributed to evil motives. And we, too, will attribute evil to other people as we misread their motives and misinterpret their words and actions.

Is there any way to prevent these relational messes, to disarm them before somebody gets hurt? Thankfully, yes. As far as our part is concerned, we can do several things.

- *Speak clearly.* This seems so basic, but many of us often give vague, unclear, and ambiguous messages. Take time to think about what you want to say, then take your time in saying it well. This can go a long way toward preventing miscommunication.

- *Listen actively.* If you aren't sure you understand what another person has said, ask questions. Rephrase what they have said, and ask them if that's right. Work patiently to make sure you're tracking with the other person.

- *Don't jump to conclusions.* For some of us, this is the best exercise we get! However, the relational damage it does outweighs any aerobic benefits. If something has been said or done when you were not present, if possible, go to the people personally and find out the facts. If that's not possible, then try to think of some kinder alternative motives and meanings than the ones you are tempted to jump to.

- *Avoid thinking the worst about the other person.* While some people will want to deliberately harm us and may indeed have ulterior motives, few people are evil incarnate. To keep from misjudging others and exaggerating their flaws, try to root your perceptions in what you know about them historically. What are they usually like? What have you observed about their character over time? If they usually operate with integrity and kindness, then chances are they are still living that way. Give them the benefit of the doubt. Try to think the best of them.

- *Remember that you're not omniscient.* You can't know everything about another person; you cannot read another's heart. Our human understanding is limited and flawed. So leave the judging up to God.

Do you need to put some of these tips into action? Write down a few particulars of your situation and what you need to do. And above all, remember that God loves you both and is the source of truth.

_____

_____

Digging Deeper

As Christians, is it really appropriate for us to ask God to deal with people who hurt us the way David did with his enemies? Is it proper for us to wish that "burning coals fall upon them . . . [that] they be cast into the fire, Into deep pits from which they cannot rise" (Ps. 140:10)? If we are supposed to turn the other cheek and love and pray for our enemies (Matt. 5:39–44), how can we pray psalms like these?

These types of lament psalms are called *imprecatory psalms*. They "contain verbalizations to God of anger at others."[7] They often rail at enemies and bring down curses on them—two features that have caused such respected Christians as C. S. Lewis to call these psalms "terrible" and "contemptible" and the writers of them sinful![8]

Are they? Are these psalms any less inspired than the rest of Scripture? Not at all. What these psalms reveal is a God-given yearning for things to be put right. For right to prevail over wrong, for justice to triumph over corruptness, for good to win over evil. Deep down, they point to the hope of God's fully realized kingdom, when Satan will be destroyed and sin won't work its damage anymore. When life will be as God originally designed it. Even Lewis concedes that

> the ferocious parts of the Psalms serve as a reminder
> that there is in the world such a thing as wickedness
> and that it . . . is hateful to God.[9]

These psalms were written, not because the writers were mad that they didn't get their way, but because real wrong had been

7. Gordon D. Fee and Douglas Stuart, *How to Read the Bible for All Its Worth* (Grand Rapids, Mich.: Zondervan Publishing House, Academie Books, 1982), p. 182.

8. C. S. Lewis, *Reflections on the Psalms* (New York, N.Y.: Harcourt, Brace and World, 1958), pp. 21–22, 26, 31–32.

9. Lewis, *Reflections on the Psalms*, p. 33.

committed against them. Their good had been repaid with evil (Ps. 35:12); they had been assaulted with lies (58:3); they had been attacked though innocent (59:3–4); their country had been threatened by nations who hated God (83:1–4); their love had been returned with hate (109:4–5); and their people had been betrayed and brutalized into captivity (Ps. 137). Their pain was real; and so was their anger.

And they were honest about it.

Are we? Sometimes we try to be "spiritual" by denying our feelings of rage and vengeance, hiding them under a veneer of Christian "niceness." We "try to jump too quickly from" conflict to resolution, "omitting the necessary but treacherous journey in between, sentimentalizing pain and praise in the process."[10]

Is God fooled? Of course not. What these psalms can do for us is "harness our anger and help us express it. . . . They guide or channel our anger *to and through* God verbally, rather than to or at anyone else, verbally or physically."[11] Rather than taking matters into our own hands, we can, as the psalmists did, bring our anger and pain and desire for revenge to God—and leave it with Him. Then—only after we have been honest with ourselves and with Him—He can help us learn to pray for those who hurt us, to show them mercy, and to "overcome evil with good" (Rom. 12:20–21).

So yes, we most certainly can pray these psalms, recognizing that their emotions are our emotions . . . and that their trust and hope in the righteous and compassionate God who "will maintain the cause of the afflicted And justice for the poor" (Ps. 140:12) can be our trust and hope too.

10. Kathleen Norris, *The Cloister Walk* (New York, N.Y.: Riverhead Books, 1996), p. 94.

11. Fee and Stuart, *How to Read the Bible for All Its Worth*, p. 182.

Chapter 4

GROWING THROUGH LOSS
Job 1–2

*B*ridge to Terabithia is a story of a deep friendship between a young boy and girl. Although they came from different backgrounds, their hearts were knit together in a secret kingdom of their own creation called Terabithia. Like all of us, they both longed for a friend who "you did everything with and told everything to."[1] And like a lucky few of us, they found it.

One day, the rope that swung them over a creek from their ordinary world to the shores of their enchanted land broke. The eleven-year-old queen of Terabithia drowned—and Jesse, her king, had to learn how to continue growing through his loss.

The story of Terabithia grew out of an event in real life; the author's eight-year-old son lost his best friend when she was struck by lightning. Katherine Paterson shares about her son's subsequent struggle to grow through this loss in a later book, *Gates of Excellence*.

> He is not fully healed. Perhaps he will never be, and I am beginning to believe that this is right. How many people in their whole lifetimes have a friend who is to them what Lisa was to David? When you have had such a gift, should you ever forget it? Of course he will forget a little. Even now he is making other friendships. His life will go on, though hers could not. And selfishly I want his pain to ease. But how can I say that I want him to "get over it," as though having loved and been loved were some sort of disease? I want the joy of knowing Lisa and the sorrow of losing her to be a part of him and to shape him into growing levels of caring and understanding, perhaps as an artist, but certainly as a person.[2]

Maybe you, too, know what it's like to have your life molded by the pressure and pain of loss. If so, there's someone you should

---

1. Katherine Paterson, *Gates of Excellence* (New York, N.Y.: Elsevier-Dutton Publishing Co., 1981), p. 96.

2. Paterson, *Gates of Excellence*, pp. 97–98.

meet: Job. Meet him in the brutal ring of suffering recorded in the first two chapters of his book, where he gets hit with incredible losses not unlike some of our own. Perhaps there with Job, in the deep intimacy of shared hurt, we can learn something that will show us how to grow through loss.

Three Key Facts about Experiencing Loss

To better understand and appreciate our own reaction to loss, as well as Job's, we first need to examine three key facts.

Categories of Loss

When we speak of loss, we can run through a gamut of meanings from trivial to serious, from losing our balance or courage to losing our will to live or even our souls (see Mark 8:36). So to help focus our understanding, let's zero in on two major categories.

First is the loss of *significant individuals*. At one time or another, all of us will be baptized into this experience either by death or by distance. Death may administer its last rites through illness, an accident, old age, war, or miscarriage. Distance may separate no less brutally through misunderstandings, divorce, or the waning intimacy of a friend who has moved away.

Second is the loss of *personal necessities or benefits*. Maybe you've walked through the charred ruins of a burned home, or felt the violation of a burglary, or gone through the grief of letting a long-time dream die. Perhaps you've been hit with sudden unemployment or had the loss of a business or your health drain the financial resources of a lifetime.

The losses may be different between the two categories, but the feelings often share the same intensity.

Reactions to Loss

Most of us are probably familiar with the stages of grief Elisabeth Kübler-Ross identified so many years ago in her insightful and compassionate book *On Death and Dying*.[3] First, when we pass through the initial shock and numbness, we enter denial—our hearts and minds struggle against the finality of our loss. When we cannot maintain our denial any longer, our anger flares and often scorches

---

3. Elisabeth Kübler-Ross, *On Death and Dying* (New York, N.Y.: Macmillan Publishing Co., 1969), chaps 3–7.

everyone around us. We even rage at God, shouting such questions at Him as, *Why me? Is this Your idea of love?*

Then we back off from our anger and try to make a bargain with God—we think that if we're good or if we promise to go to that mission field, maybe He'll prevent, postpone, or somehow undo the loss. When our attempts at making deals are exhausted, we sink into depression. Pain is our constant companion, and hope seems ever out of our reach. Time drags, tiredness weighs us down, and life looks flat and meaningless. When we finally emerge from depression's dark tunnel, the peace of accepting the loss helps us regain our equilibrium and engage life once again.

Ideally, this is how we will progress through grief and grow through the process. Not all of us, however, experience the ideal.

Some of us respond to loss with bitterness. We slam shut the doors of our heart, we continue to nurse our anger at God, and we retreat into cynicism. If we allow this hardness to persist, it can sour into a lifetime of resentment. Without God and without hope, this is the best some people manage to do.

With God and with His hope, though (see 1 Thess. 4:13–14), we can indeed come to accept our loss and mature into more compassionate people whose faith in God has deepened. Our pain can be transformed into peace and understanding, and we will be able to smile at life again.

Perspective

Our perspective can have a lot to do with how we cope with grief. First, we need to realize that grieving is not "un-Christian." It's a normal part of the human experience, an appropriate response to loss, that Jesus Himself shared (see John 11). Second, we need to fix our eyes on the Lord, as Jesus did, so we can look beyond the anguish and the disappointment and know the realness of hope. When we honestly acknowledge our grief and ask God to walk with us through each of its stages, then we can move through it with measured steps toward growth and maturity.

Job: A Classic Case Study

Now let's enter into Job's world, feeling what he lost and learning from his response.

What He Had

Beginning in Job 1:1, we are given a personal inventory of Job's spiritual and material wealth. At the top of that list is Job's own personal character. His godliness came from a genuine, committed walk with God (see also vv. 4–5).

The list continues with the blessings of children (v. 2), wealth and servants (v. 3a), and prestige (v. 3b). It's easy to think that life was always like this for Job. We forget that he, too, went through the trials of raising ten children, building a successful business, and cultivating a love for God in the midst of it all. Remembering this may help us identify with him better as we turn our attention from what he possessed to what he lost.

What He Lost

Satan was sure that Job followed God only because of His blessings; if they were taken away, he contended, Job's faith in God would dissolve. To prove the integrity of His servant, God allowed the growing pain of loss to be brought upon Job.[4]

> Now on the day when his sons and his daughters were eating and drinking wine in their oldest brother's house, a messenger came to Job and said, "The oxen were plowing and the donkeys feeding beside them, and the Sabeans attacked and took them. They also slew the servants with the edge of the sword, and I alone have escaped to tell you." *While he was still speaking,* another also came and said, "The fire of God fell from heaven and burned up the sheep and the servants and consumed them, and I alone have escaped to tell you." *While he was still speaking,* another also came and said, "The Chaldeans formed three bands and made a raid on the camels and took them and slew the servants with the edge of the sword, and I alone have escaped to tell you." *While he was still speaking,* another also came and said, "Your sons and your daughters were eating and drinking wine in their oldest brother's

---

4. All losses are not necessarily because of some wrong. In Job's case, it was his blameless character and faith, not sin, that prompted his being tested by grievous losses.

house, and behold, a great wind came from across
the wilderness and struck the four corners of the
house, and it fell on the young people and they died,
and I alone have escaped to tell you." (Job 1:13–19,
emphasis added)

As Alexander Whyte poignantly observed, "Job's sorrows came
not in single spies, but in battalions."[5] The children he had prayed
for and all he had worked for were brutally torn out of his life
completely and in an instant.

How It Happened

Satan didn't send up any warning flags so that Job could prepare
himself. He just came up behind Job and hit him with all the
meanness and power he could put into a blow. Job's wealth and
family were utterly devastated; nothing could be recovered.

How He Reacted

Job's reaction to having everything stripped away from him was
pretty disappointing . . . for Satan.

Then Job arose and tore his robe and shaved his
head, and he fell to the ground and worshiped. He
said,
"Naked I came from my mother's womb,
And naked I shall return there.
The Lord gave and the Lord has taken away.
Blessed be the name of the Lord."
Through all this Job did not sin nor did he blame
God. (vv. 20–22)

Author Mike Mason helps us more deeply appreciate Job's words
and actions.

He shows himself at the outset to be a man for whom
worship is second nature. . . . Worship is his initial
response, worship is the spontaneous reaction to trag-
edy that wells up out of his soul, and somehow everything he says later on must be judged in the light of

---

5. Alexander Whyte, *Bible Characters: The Old Testament* (London, England: Oliphants;
Grand Rapids, Mich.: Zondervan Publishing House, 1952), vol. 1, p. 379.

this fact. For we know that under such circumstances worship does not come to a person naturally or spontaneously, but rather it is a practiced response, a fruit of long faith and discipline. Job could never have reacted as he did unless he had been practicing for this moment all his life.

Before we consider the actual words of Job's worship, we need to pause and take careful note of the attitude of heart in which they were offered. Was Job, in the midst of his grief and turmoil, somehow at peace? Was he filled with a strange spiritual joy? No, not at all. He was as broken and cast down as a man can be.[6]

Yet Job worshiped God (v. 20), humbly acknowledging His sovereign right to do as He wanted with his life (v. 21). Job "assumed no inherent right to his possessions. ... . [And] he did not pursue any course of action to cope with his losses that would blemish his faith in God"[7] (v. 22). We, too, need to be careful that we don't build up the unrealistic expectation that God's blessings—whether people or material things—are ours to keep for all our lives. He is the owner; we are only the stewards. He is first, and He is worthy of worship in all situations.

Did Job's faithful response satisfy Satan? No, it only made him more vicious.

> "Skin for skin! Yes, all that a man has he will give for his life. However, put forth Your hand now, and touch his bone and his flesh; he will curse You to Your face." So the Lord said to Satan, "Behold, he is in your power, only spare his life."
>
> Then Satan went out from the presence of the Lord and smote Job with sore boils from the sole of

6. Mike Mason, *The Gospel According to Job* (Wheaton, Ill.: Good News Publishers, Crossway Books, 1994), p. 35.

7. John E. Hartley, *The Book of Job*, The New International Commentary on the Old Testament series, gen. ed. R. K. Harrison (Grand Rapids, Mich.: William B. Eerdmans Publishing Co., 1988), p. 78.

his foot to the crown of his head.[8] And he took a
potsherd to scrape himself while he was sitting
among the ashes. (2:4–8)

Despite his miserable physical condition and his grief, Job con-
tinued to trust God. But his wife was struggling in her pain—
remember, all his losses were hers too, and she could only watch
helplessly as her husband suffered. Her words, unfortunately, were
no help to Job.

> Then his wife said to him, "Do you still hold
> fast your integrity? Curse God and die!" (v. 9)

Was she angry with God? Blaming Job for a hidden sin that
had brought all this misery about? Or did she want to end his pain
quickly with a lightning bolt from God? We don't know. But "according to her view, to compromise one's faith in God in order to
ease an intolerable burden is the wisest course to follow."[9] How
deeply this must have hurt Job, to now be alienated from his wife
in the midst of his sufferings. He held fast to his faith, though, and
corrected her foolish talk.

> But he said to her, "You speak as one of the foolish
> women speaks. Shall we indeed accept good from
> God and not accept adversity?" In all this Job did
> not sin with his lips. (v. 10)

Job's question, "Shall we accept good from God and not accept
adversity?" gives us one of the most profound thoughts in Scripture.
Once again, Mike Mason illuminates this for us.

> Job refuses . . . to get bogged down in trying
> to understand all the "reasons" for his misfortune.

---

8. Job's affliction looked like the plagues in the curses pronounced on the disobedient in
Deuteronomy 28:27, 35. Perhaps that's why, later in the book, his friends attribute his
condition to some sin of his. What, precisely, was Job's disease? Commentators have proposed
everything from leprosy to elephantiasis to diabetes mellitus, but no one can know for certain.
"From Job's speeches some of the symptoms that he suffered included painful pruritus [severe
itching] (2:8), disfiguration (2:12), purulent [pus-filled] sores that scab over, crack, and ooze
(7:5), sores infected with worms (7:5), fever with chills (21:6; 30:30), darkening and shriv-
eling of the skin (30:30), eyes red and swollen from weeping (16:16), diarrhea (30:27),
sleeplessness and delirium (7:4, 13–14), choking (7:15), bad breath (19:17), emaciation
(19:20), and excruciating pain throughout his body (30:17)." Hartley, *The Book of Job*, p. 82

9. Hartley, *The Book of Job*, p. 84.

God knows the reasons; he does not. To "accept trouble from God" implies the acceptance of a certain illogical dimension to life, a dimension so totally beyond human ken that even faith, by its own secret and darkly luminous wisdom, cannot really comprehend it. . . .

It is much easier to use one's mind to reduce God to understandable proportions than it is continually to accommodate oneself to the divine mystery. It is easier to diminish God than to enlarge one's own heart. . . .

In some way Job's wise and simple words in 2:10 are the very last expression of clear-minded, unshaken faith that he will utter before he sinks completely beneath the waves. . . . After this point in the story Job's suffering at the hands of Satan grows so intense and prolonged that everything he says will be laced with darkness and confusion, so that at times his very character will appear to have come unhinged. Yet however much this man's humble faith may seem to be dashed to pieces later on, here at the outset we see him as he really is. We see him, in spite of terrible strain and agony, still in his right mind, and we realize that here is a person whose nature was not characteristically of a pessimistic, brooding or morbid type, but rather steadfast and sanguine.[10]

Lessons from a Seasoned Sufferer

As we leave Job and turn to face the painful losses in our own lives, let's remember three important lessons.

First, *our major goal in life is not to be happy or satisfied but to glorify God.* This idea cuts across the grain of the human mind-set, which says happiness is our inalienable right and chief goal in life. But how truly happy can we be if we ignore or walk away from God? His goal is not that we should never experience trials but that by them we should be conformed to His image and bring Him glory (see Rom. 8:29; 1 Cor. 10:31).

---

10. Mason, *The Gospel According to Job,* pp. 47–48.

Second, *the path of obedience is marked by times of loss and suffering.* The presence of pain does not automatically mean that we are being punished for being disobedient. God has reasons for shaping our lives the way He does that we can never conceive or understand. Remember, no one was more obedient to God than Jesus, and think of how He suffered. We can be in the center of God's will, like Job and Jesus, and still all hell may break loose against us. So don't judge yourself or others by the hard times that hit.

Third, *what is considered loss now often leads to gain later.* At the end of Job's story, God gave him ten more children and restored in double all his wealth (Job 42:12–13). His greatest gain, though, as for all who suffer a loss and continue trusting God, was in glorifying God and knowing Him even more deeply than before.

> But whatever things were gain to me, those things I have counted as loss for the sake of Christ. More than that, I count all things to be loss in view of the surpassing value of knowing Christ Jesus my Lord, for whom I have suffered the loss of all things, and count them but rubbish so that I may gain Christ. (Phil. 3:7–8)

❧ *Living Insights*

A little further along in Job's story, three of his friends come to "sympathize with him and comfort him" (Job 2:11). Though they actually did him much harm later, at first they behaved very wisely. They took on his pain as if it were their own—weeping, tearing their robes, and sprinkling dust on their heads. But most importantly,

> They sat down on the ground with him for seven days and seven nights with no one speaking a word to him, for they saw that his pain was very great. (v. 13)

Sometimes the best thing we can do for someone who is reeling with pain is just be with them. Silently. Our care and love can often best be shown in our wordless presence—in an embrace, in tears. Craig Dykstra explains why this is so much more effective than our words.

> Presence is a service of vulnerability. To be present to others is to put oneself in the position of being

vulnerable to what they are vulnerable to, and of being vulnerable to them. It means being willing to suffer what the other suffers, and to go with the sufferer in his or her own suffering. This is different from trying to become the sufferer. Presence does not involve taking another's place. That would be demeaning. It would suggest, "I can take your suffering better than you can, so move aside; I will replace you." Instead, presence involves exposing oneself to what the sufferer is exposed to, and being with the other in that vulnerability.[11]

If you can, try to give the gift of your presence to those who are hurting. And when you hurt, seek out those who can sit in sensitive silence with you. It will begin to bring healing to your heart and relief to your soul.

11. Craig Dykstra, *Vision and Character* (Mahwah, N.J.: Paulist Press, 1981), p. 102; as quoted by David Atkinson, *The Message of Job: Suffering and Grace*, The Bible Speaks Today Series (Downers Grove, Ill.: InterVarsity Press, 1991), pp. 30–31.

Chapter 5

GROWING THROUGH MISTAKES
Psalm 31

*O*ops! . . . *Rats*. . . . *Darn it!* . . . *Uh-oh*. . . . *Oh shoot!*
. . . *Crud*. . . . *Oohh nooo!*

Hmm. Sounds like somebody's been making a pile of mistakes. It wasn't me! (This time.) Was it you?

All of us make mistakes; it's just part of being human. But it's one of the tougher parts of being human, isn't it? Because making mistakes is often embarrassing, humbling, sometimes even humiliating. After all, who likes to look incompetent?

And so often, our mistakes are out there for everybody to see. Architect Frank Lloyd Wright once quipped, "The physician can bury his mistakes, but the architect can only advise his clients to plant vines."[1] We don't mind the little mistakes so much, like forgetting that now-charred batch of cookies in the oven or forgetting to pay the electric bill on time. But the big ones, the tragic ones, can bring on shame and haunting guilt.

Where do you hide when you've lost your life savings because of an unwise business decision? When you've impulsively entered into a marriage that turns out to be disastrous? When you've prescribed the wrong medication and put someone in a coma? When you didn't see your child as you backed out of the driveway?

There's only one place to hide, one place to begin again—in the shelter of God's love. If you've made a big, heartbreaking mistake and don't know how you'll survive, or if you're just weary of all the messes your smaller mistakes have put you in, then this chapter is for you. Let's open God's Word and find the hope and strength He offers in our times of need.

---

1. Frank Lloyd Wright, *New York Times Magazine*, October 4, 1953, as quoted in Microsoft Bookshelf 98, copyright © 1987–1997 Microsoft Corporation. All rights reserved. From *The Columbia Dictionary of Quotations*, licensed from Columbia University Press. Copyright © 1993, 1995 by Columbia University Press. All rights reserved.

Mistakes Happen

Before we go on, it will help us to understand precisely what a mistake is. Is a mistake a sin? Not necessarily. Because we live in an imperfect, fallen world and are imperfect, fallen people, we will make mistakes. But sin is more deliberate; we know something is wrong and choose it purposely. The dictionary, in contrast, defines *mistake* as

> [verb] to blunder in the choice of . . . to misunderstand the meaning or intention of: misinterpret . . . to make a wrong judgment of the character or ability of . . . to identify wrongly: confuse with another . . . to be wrong. . . . [noun] a misunderstanding of the meaning or implication of something . . . a wrong action or statement proceeding from faulty judgment, inadequate knowledge, or inattention.[2]

Mistakes, then, are not out-and-out rebellion, deception, or willful disobedience. Those things are intentional and are clearly sinful. Mistakes can sometimes lead to sin, but on the whole they are accidental or blundering in nature and stem from a variety of motives. Let's take a look at a few of them.

- *Panic-prompted mistakes.* Panic-prompted mistakes spring from fear, hurry, or worry. They come from wrong decisions made with only a desperate, split-second thought. We often make this type of mistake in the area of romance. Yearning for love, we may cling to the first person who comes along, afraid that no one else will ever come and we'll live out our lives alone.

- *Well-intentioned mistakes.* Have you ever tried to do the right thing but at the wrong time or in the wrong way? Your motives were pure, but your method was off, and your words or actions resulted in an embarrassing gaffe. "So, when is your baby due?" you ask with a gentle, I'm-excited-for-you smile. Only to receive a glare and a terse answer, "I'm not pregnant." Oops.

- *Negligent mistakes.* Inattentiveness and carelessness can also prompt mistakes. When we don't bother to look in the rearview mirror but just blithely change lanes, we can make a costly—and potentially fatal—error.

2. *Merriam-Webster's Collegiate Dictionary*, 10th ed., see "mistake."

- *Unrestrained-curiosity mistakes.* Curiosity, that desire in us to investigate and learn and know, is often a good thing, a key that opens many doors to understanding the people and the world around us. However, when curiosity becomes a guiding force of its own with no regard for safety and discernment, it can lead us into making some regrettable mistakes. How many chain smokers, for example, wish they'd never wondered what a cigarette was like?

- *Blind-spot mistakes.* Blind-spot mistakes happen because, well, because we have blind spots. We're ignorant about a lot of things, and sometimes we don't exercise very good judgment because we rely on ingrained habits and unchallenged perceptions. For instance, a woman may choose the same type of charming but self-absorbed man over and over again, winding up feeling alone and uncared for, because she does not see what she is doing. She's blind to the fact that she keeps choosing men who are like her father.

All the above and more—rash decisions, being too nice, jumping to conclusions (just to name a few)—can cause mistakes. Because we're human, we'll always slip up somewhere. Fortunately, God "is mindful that we are but dust" (Ps. 103:14)—fashioned by His hands, dependent on His care. And His care and love are here in abundance for us, no matter what we've done or failed to do.

Recovery Happens Too

In Psalm 31, we find David in trouble. Enemies have surrounded him, schemed against him, slandered him. But notice, David does not make the mistake of striking back at them, of taking care of business in his own strength. Instead, he seeks the Lord, his shelter.

Often, our mistakes can feel like enemies, raining down embarrassment and shame, proclaiming our foolishness from the rooftops. The agony of their consequences can seem inescapable. We, too, need a refuge, a redeemer. And that's just what we'll find in the inspired images of God that David provides in this psalm.

God, Our Refuge

David begins his psalm with a prayer:

In You, O Lord, I have taken refuge;
Let me never be ashamed;

In Your righteousness deliver me.
Incline Your ear to me, rescue me quickly;
Be to me a rock of strength,
A stronghold to save me.
For You are my rock and my fortress;
For Your name's sake You will lead me and guide me.
You will pull me out of the net which they have
    secretly laid for me,
For You are my strength.
Into Your hand I commit my spirit;
You have ransomed me, O Lord, God of truth.
(vv. 1–5)

Notice what David depends on God to be for him: a refuge (a safe, welcoming place), a righteous deliverer (a perfect and caring Savior), a rock of strength and a fortress (a sure and solid protection). David can trust that God will come through for him, so he is not ashamed to put his faith in Him (v. 1). "Even in his great need," commentator Willem A. VanGemeren tells us,

> the psalmist has not lost heart, because he knows his God. His trust in the Lord is an act of abandonment: "Into your hands I commit my spirit" (v. 5).[3]

Recognize this last phrase? Jesus spoke these words on the cross (Luke 23:46), giving Himself wholly into His Father's hands. When trouble surrounds us, even if it comes at our own hands, God would still have us give ourselves to Him. He is worthy of our trust, because no one loves us better than He does.

God, Who Sees and Loves Us

David next affirms his trust in the Lord.

I hate those who regard vain idols,
But I trust in the Lord.
I will rejoice and be glad in Your lovingkindness,
Because You have seen my affliction;
You have known the troubles of my soul,

---

3. Willem A. VanGemeren, "Psalms," in *The Expositor's Bible Commentary*, gen. ed. Frank E. Gaebelein (Grand Rapids, Mich.: Zondervan Publishing House, 1991), vol. 5, p. 264.

And You have not given me over into the hand of
    the enemy;
You have set my feet in a large place.
(Ps. 31:6–8)

God sees us, knows us—all about us—and does not abandon
us. In His love, He protects us and gives us breathing room.[4] When
we are reeling in the wake of a bad mistake, rejection and aban-
donment are two things we fear most. What a comfort it is to know
that God will not abandon us— He will set us in a safe place where
we can regain our footing.

God, Whom We Can Trust

In verses 9–13, David details the distress he's in and casts himself on God's grace. "My eye is wasted away from grief . . . my life
is spent with sorrow" (vv. 9, 10). Yet, despite his pain and weariness,
he steadfastly trusts in God because he is anchored in God's goodness.

But as for me, I trust in You, O Lord,
I say, "You are my God."
My times are in Your hand;
Deliver me from the hand of my enemies and from
    those who persecute me.
Make Your face to shine upon Your servant;
Save me in Your lovingkindness.
Let me not be put to shame, O Lord, for I call
    upon You;
Let the wicked be put to shame, let them be silent
    in Sheol.
Let the lying lips be mute,
Which speak arrogantly against the righteous
With pride and contempt.
How great is Your goodness,
Which You have stored up for those who fear You,
Which You have wrought for those who take refuge
    in You,
Before the sons of men!
You hide them in the secret place of Your presence

---

4. Eugene Peterson, in *The Message: The Wisdom Books*, renders verse 8 like this: "You didn't
leave me in [my tormentors'] clutches but gave me room to breathe" (Colorado Springs,
Colo.: NavPress, 1996), p. 124.

from the conspiracies of man;
You keep them secretly in a shelter from the strife
of tongues.
Blessed be the Lord,
For He has made marvelous His lovingkindness to
me in a besieged city.
As for me, I said in my alarm,
"I am cut off from before Your eyes";
Nevertheless You heard the voice of my supplications
When I cried to You. (vv. 14–22)

All of our times are in God's hands (v. 15)—both good and
bad, pleasant and unpleasant, wise and foolish. And when we turn
to Him in faith, He turns to us with radiant love (v. 16). When
we are hemmed in, He bestows kindness on us (v. 21). When we
think we're beyond help, He listens and compassionately responds
to our cries (v. 22).

God, Our Hope

With a God who cares about us so much and loves us so actively,
even we mistake-prone people can have hope!

O love the Lord, all you His godly ones!
The Lord preserves the faithful
And fully recompenses the proud doer.
Be strong and let your heart take courage,
All you who hope in the Lord. (vv. 23–24)

Be strong, you who are human and err; let your heart take
courage. God won't erase consequences, but He has a new day for
each of us—a new start with each sunrise and a new heavenly day
when we'll finally be beyond our mistakes. And won't that be a
great day!

🌺 *Living Insights*

"Experience," playwright Oscar Wilde observed, "is the name
everyone gives to their mistakes."[5] Do you ever feel like you are

5. Oscar Wilde, as quoted in *Bartlett's Familiar Quotations*, 15th ed., rev. and enl., ed. Emily
Morison Beck (Boston, Mass.: Little, Brown and Co., 1980), p. 675.

too "experienced"? If you'd like to do all you can to prevent mistakes, here are three tips:

- Check your motive—ask yourself why you're going to do what you're about to do.

- Check the moment—think about the timing of what you're about to do.

- Check the method—determine if this is the best way to do what you are about to do.

Then, when (not if) you make another mistake, remember that you're human and do your best to learn from that mistake. Ask God's help—He's for you, not against you. And seek His guidance in putting things right. He's in the business of making all things new.

Chapter 6

GROWING THROUGH WEAKNESS

Psalm 46

The lady was tired.

Not physically tired, though she had worked a full day; nor tired from age—she was only forty-two. No, she was tired of being treated with disrespect. Tired of seeing her people being treated like second-class citizens. Tired of giving in to injustice and bigotry.

So when the bus driver told her row of four passengers, "Let me have those seats"—to make room for one white man—she did not move.

"Y'all better make it light on yourselves and let me have those seats," the bus driver repeated. The other three got up and moved, but she did not. Instead, she slid closer to the window. A woman should not have to give up her seat for a man, she thought; and besides, they all paid the same ten cents to ride the bus.

Once more, the bus driver asked her if she was going to move. "No," was her reply.

"Well, I'm going to have you arrested," he stated.

"You may do that," she answered, and he did.[1] Though they didn't realize it at the time, a turning point in United States history had arrived. For the lady's name was Rosa Parks, and her David-like resistance to the Goliath of racial segregation sparked the Montgomery bus boycott, which helped fuel the Civil Rights movement throughout the nation.

Outnumbered, overpowered, and with a whole legal system slanted unjustly against her, Rosa Parks nevertheless let God take her weak position and turn it into colossal strength. Of this experience she writes,

I had no idea that history was being made. I was

---

1. Rosa Parks, with Jim Haskins, *Rosa Parks: My Story* (New York, N.Y.: Dial Books, 1992), pp. 113–17; Rosa Parks, with Gregory J. Reed, *Quiet Strength: The Faith, the Hope, and the Heart of a Woman Who Changed a Nation* (Grand Rapids, Mich.: Zondervan Publishing House, 1994), pp. 21–23.

just tired of giving in. Somehow, I felt that what I did was right by standing up to that bus driver. I did not think about the consequences. I knew that I could have been lynched, manhandled, or beaten when the police came. I chose not to move. . . .

There were other people on the bus whom I knew. But when I was arrested, not one of them came to my defense. I felt very much alone. One man who knew me did not even go by my house to tell my husband I had been arrested. Everyone just went on their way.

In jail I felt even more alone. For a moment, as I sat in that little room with bars, before I was moved to a cell with two other women, I felt that I had been deserted. . . .

. . . Getting arrested was one of the worst days in my life. . . . Since I have always been a strong believer in God, I knew that He was with me, and only He could get me through.[2]

And He did. He will see us through as well, when we feel completely outmatched by life's challenges. Because God cares for the weak; in fact, He has even "chosen the weak things of the world to shame the things which are strong" (1 Cor. 1:27). Might does not make right in God's economy. But His righteousness makes mighty those who trust in Him.

When We Are Weak . . .

In our survival-of-the-fittest world, compassion and care for the weak are not usually a high priority. Rather, the powerful often look on the weak with contempt, as these withering words from actress Bette Davis reveal: "The weak are the most treacherous of us all. They come to the strong and drain them. They are bottomless. They are insatiable. They are always parched and always bitter. They are everyone's concern and like vampires they suck our life's blood."[3]

2. Parks and Reed, *Quiet Strength*, pp. 23–24.

3. Bette Davis, *The Lonely Life* (1962), chap. 20. As quoted in Microsoft Bookshelf 98, copyright © and ℗ 1987–1996 Microsoft Corporation. All rights reserved. From *The Columbia Dictionary of Quotations*, licensed from Columbia University Press. Copyright © 1995 by Columbia University Press. All rights reserved.

It would be hard to get much further from God's heart than that! And it would be hard to find a human being who was not weak at some time in his or her life. Even the apostle Paul, a seeming lion among the apostles, was buffeted by weakness.

> Five times I received from the Jews thirty-nine lashes. Three times I was beaten with rods, once I was stoned, three times I was shipwrecked, a night and a day I have spent in the deep. I have been on frequent journeys, in dangers from rivers, dangers from robbers, dangers from my countrymen, dangers from the Gentiles, dangers in the city, dangers in the wilderness, dangers on the sea, dangers among false brethren; I have been in labor and hardship, through many sleepless nights, in hunger and thirst, often without food, in cold and exposure. Apart from such external things, there is the daily pressure on me of concern for all the churches. Who is weak without my being weak? (2 Cor. 11:24–29a)

In addition to these, Paul struggled with a physical infirmity, his "thorn in the flesh," which God would not remove despite his pleading (12:7–8). Yet, rather than feeling disqualified, unworthy, or ashamed of all that was against him, Paul boasted in his weakness (11:30; 12:9)! Why? Because God said to him,

> "My grace is sufficient for you, for power is perfected in weakness." Most gladly, therefore, I will rather boast about my weaknesses, so that the power of Christ may dwell in me. Therefore I am well content with weaknesses, with insults, with distresses, with persecutions, with difficulties, for Christ's sake; for when I am weak, then I am strong. (vv. 9–10)

When we are weak, God fills us with His strength. Our vulnerability is the backdrop for the display of His power—an open door for His might to be released and brought to fulfillment in our lives. Unlike the world, God deals graciously with us when we are helpless and frail.

He also treats us with tenderness and compassion, as this prophecy concerning His Son's actions shows:

> "A bruised reed He will not break

And a dimly burning wick He will not extinguish;
He will faithfully bring forth justice." (Isa. 42:3)

And with overwhelming generosity, He exchanges our weakness
for new strength:

He gives strength to the weary,
And to him who lacks might He increases power.
Though youths grow weary and tired,
And vigorous young men stumble badly,
Yet those who wait for the Lord
Will gain new strength;
They will mount up with wings like eagles,
They will run and not get tired,
They will walk and not become weary.
(Isa. 40:29–31)

How gracious, tender, and generous God is with us when we
trust Him in our weakness. There's no safer place we can go, no
surer help we can find.

. . . He Is Strong

When we're outnumbered and unprotected, when our hearts
tremble and we're shaken to the core, God remains steady, strong,
and secure. That's what Psalm 46 celebrates—God's deliverance in
troubled times.[4] Let's turn to this inspired portrait of our Lord to
learn of His strength, His help, and His victory, and how He can
help us when we are weak.

We Need Not Fear

The psalm begins with an expression of deep trust.

God is our refuge and strength,
A very present help in trouble.
Therefore we will not fear, though the earth should
change

---

4. The superscription of this psalm says, "For the choir director. A Psalm of the sons of
Korah, set to Alamoth. A Song." *Alamoth* possibly means "for soprano voices," according to
the NASB margin note. However, no women's choir is mentioned in the Old Testament,
so this may refer to instruments tuned to a maiden-like, or high-pitched, tone. Also note
the use of *Selah*, which might have signaled a pause for reflection or a crescendo for emphasis
after each stanza of the psalm.

And though the mountains slip into the heart of
    the sea;
Though its waters roar and foam,
Though the mountains quake at its swelling pride.
(vv. 1–3)

"God is a safe place to hide," Eugene Peterson paraphrases,
"ready to help when we need him."[5] If all of creation should heave
and pitch, returning to the formlessness from which it was brought
forth, we need not fear. God shelters us; He is very near and brings
help to us in His outstretched hands.

We Will Not Be Moved

Next, the psalm prophetically pictures the security of the city
protected by God.

There is a river whose streams make glad the city
    of God,
The holy dwelling places of the Most High.
God is in the midst of her, she will not be moved;
God will help her when morning dawns.
The nations made an uproar, the kingdoms tottered;
He raised His voice, the earth melted.
The Lord of hosts is with us;
The God of Jacob is our stronghold. (vv. 4–7)

The waters of life and healing will flow through God's city (see
Ezek. 47:1–12; Rev. 22:1–2), replicating the refreshment and joy
of the Garden of Eden. The Lord Himself will live in that city with
His people, sustaining and defending them. The nations may gather
to attack at dawn, but with just the sound of His voice, God can
make the earth melt. What enemy can oppose Him? Surely, He
and His heavenly host will protect us, and in the stronghold of His
care, we will not be moved or shaken.

We Don't Need to Strive

"Come, behold the works of the Lord," the psalm next urges
(Ps. 46:8a). Look at what God has done, and consider it well,
because "the recitation of the mighty acts of God plants deep in

5. Eugene H. Peterson, *The Message: The Wisdom Books* (Colorado Springs, Colo.: NavPress,
1996), p. 149.

the memory of God's people the evidences of his care, protection, and providential rule."[6] What has the Lord done?

> [He] has wrought desolations in the earth.
> He makes wars to cease to the end of the earth;
> He breaks the bow and cuts the spear in two;
> He burns the chariots with fire. (vv. 8b–9)

God's "desolations" are the horrors brought about by His righteous judgment, meted out to people who spread evil, violence, and war over the earth. The Lord will destroy our weapons and establish lasting peace—this is His sovereign purpose. Which is why He Himself speaks in the next verse:

> "Cease striving and know that I am God;
> I will be exalted among the nations,
> I will be exalted in the earth." (v. 10)

Do you know what *cease* means here? The Hebrew word is *raphah*, meaning "sink, relax." Sink into the Lord's powerful care; relax in the knowledge that He is God and He will triumph. We don't need to strive and struggle in our weaknesses; we can rest in who God is and what He will do. Remember,

> The Lord of hosts is *with us;*
> The God of Jacob is *our stronghold.*
> (v. 11, emphasis added)

Concluding Thoughts

Are you feeling weak or overwhelmed right now? Are you wondering how you can go on? Then keep in mind these three reminders about God's strength.

- *His strength is immediately available.* He is near, a "very present help in trouble" (v. 1).

- *His power is overpowering.* There is no weakness that He cannot stretch the canopy of His power to cover.

- *His power is sufficient without our help.* He only wants us to be willing, like the apostle Paul, to know our weakness and rely on Him to provide the strength we need.

6. Willem A. VanGemeren, "Psalms," in *The Expositor's Bible Commentary,* gen. ed. Frank E. Gaebelein (Grand Rapids, Mich.: Zondervan Publishing House, 1991), vol. 5, p. 353.

Most gladly, therefore, I will rather boast about my weaknesses, so that the power of Christ may dwell in me. . . . For when I am weak, then I am strong. (2 Cor. 12:9b, 10b)

🌸 *Living Insights*

Have you ever taken the time to trace God's care for the weak through Scripture? Let's do that now. Delve into the following references, and jot down insights and applications you find. May this encourage you when you feel weak, and may it challenge you to be a channel of God's compassion to the powerless and vulnerable.

1 Samuel 2:8–9 _____

_____

_____

1 Chronicles 29:12 _____

_____

_____

Psalm 10:16–18 _____

_____

_____

Psalm 82:1–4 _____

_____

_____

Proverbs 31:8–9 _____

_____

_____

Isaiah 35:3 _____

_____

Isaiah 41:10 _____

_____

_____

Acts 20:35 _____

_____

_____

1 Corinthians 1:27 _____

_____

_____

1 Corinthians 9:22 _____

_____

_____

1 Thessalonians 5:14 _____

_____

_____

2 Thessalonians 3:3 _____

_____

_____

Hebrews 12:12 _____

_____

_____

Chapter 7

GROWING THROUGH MONOTONY

Psalm 90

"I'm so bored." Have you ever felt like your life just wasn't going anywhere? That instead of living on the fast track, you were trudging around in the same old rut? Like Sisyphus, who, in Greek mythology, was condemned eternally to roll a stone uphill only to have it roll down before he got to the top, we all feel trapped sometimes in a life of meaningless tasks. Shakespeare captured the essence of our condition:

> Life is as tedious as a twice-told tale,
> Vexing the dull ear of a drowsy man.[1]

What causes us to feel this way? Sometimes we need a challenge—we've outgrown our jobs, for example, and long for something more. Sometimes we need something new—we've "been there, done that," and life feels stale. Sometimes, though, we're bored because we feel empty. Life has become bland and tasteless because we've lost touch with its meaning. We don't sense any purpose in our activities anymore.

How do we reconnect with life's meaning when we're in the valley of monotony? How do we learn again that each day, despite its seeming sameness, is a gift from God? Let's listen to the words of a man who knew more monotony than most of us put together yet still stayed attuned to life's significance: Moses.

Observing the Psalm

Psalm 90 is Moses' sober, poignant prayer.

> Contrasting God's eternity with human transitori-
> ness, and confessing that man's days pass away in God's
> wrath, the psalmist prayed that the compassionate

---

1. William Shakespeare, *King John*, act 3, scene 4, as quoted in *Bartlett's Familiar Quotations*, 15th ed., rev. and enl., ed. Emily Morison Beck (Boston, Mass.: Little, Brown and Co., 1980), p. 202.

God would give His people success for their labors
and joy for their sorrows.[2]

This is the only psalm attributed to Moses in the book of Psalms, making it most likely the oldest psalm as well. From his somber tenor and the mention of God's wrath, Moses probably wrote it during Israel's forty years of wandering in the wilderness. Earlier in his life, Moses had spent another forty years keeping company with a herd of sheep in the Midian desert. So he knew monotony backwards and forwards, inside and out.

Though Moses' prayer is borne out of the experience of living under God's righteous wrath, we can glean some practical principles from it to help us grow through our times of monotony today.

Breaking the Spell

Often, the sing-song sameness of monotonous routines has a mesmerizing effect on our spirits. Our "inner eye" can hardly stay open, and we settle into a lethargy that leaves us sleepwalking through our days. We go through the motions, but our hearts and minds aren't in it. Breaking boredom's hold requires that we consciously direct our attention toward the Lord.

The Right Object

Moses begins his prayer by focusing on God's eternal care for His people.

Lord, You have been our dwelling place in all
generations. (Ps. 90:1)

In God, we have a secure "dwelling place," a refuge, an "oasis of refreshment and encampment."[3] Moses is reaffirming that our home is with God. For us, to be at home is to abide with Him.

When we realize that God is with us—in everything that we do—we will begin to take hold of meaning in our lives again. We will emerge from the gray fog of emptiness and recenter ourselves in God, coming home to Him. Then, even in life's most monotonous

---

2. Allen P. Ross, "Psalms," in *The Bible Knowledge Commentary*, Old Testament edition, ed. John F. Walvoord and Roy B. Zuck (Colorado Springs, Colo.: Chariot Victor Publishing, 1985), p. 859.

3. Willem A. VanGemeren, "Psalms," in *The Expositor's Bible Commentary*, gen. ed. Frank E. Gaebelein (Grand Rapids, Mich.: Zondervan Publishing House, 1991), vol. 5, p. 592.

details, we will have purpose, because our actions are grounded in the highest and deepest reality: God with us.

The Right Perspective

Moses next turns to the permanence and infinity of God.

> Before the mountains were born,
> Or You gave birth to the earth and the world,
> Even from everlasting to everlasting, You are
>   God. (v. 2)

Moses poetically broadens his perspective to see God's presence in eternity past and future. It's His presence—at all times and places—that gives our tasks, however menial, importance. It is not the size of our tasks that gives them their significance, but the size of our God.

Probing the Soul

Now Moses verbalizes three thoughts that often haunt us when we feel like our lives are being spent on a monotonous treadmill.

My Life Is So Short

In contrast to God's authority and eternal grandeur, in verses 3–6 Moses holds up a collage of pictures depicting the frailty and brevity of human life.

> You turn man back into dust
> And say, "Return, O children of men."
> For a thousand years in Your sight
> Are like yesterday when it passes by,
> Or as a watch in the night.
> You have swept them away like a flood, they fall asleep;
> In the morning they are like grass which sprouts anew.
> In the morning it flourishes and sprouts anew;
> Toward evening it fades and withers away.

God gives us life and determines our end. He creates mountains and returns us to dust. We know that "each human being is a drop in the giant stream of time,"[4] yet we yearn to make our drop last

---

4. VanGemeren, "Psalms," p. 594.

forever, don't we? We long to make a lasting mark, to do great things that people will remember. But time fades our deeds, and the specter of a short life spent attending tedious details haunts us all.

My Sins Are So Obvious

"Why should this be?" one commentator asks.

> Why should a species destined to eat of the Tree of Life and live for ever (Gn. 2:16; 3:22) crumble to dust and sleep in death? . . . [Verse] 7 gives the answer—divine *anger* . . . *indignation* against iniquities . . . *secret sins* (8), *wrath* (9)! . . . The common denominator of people worldwide is a sad tale of lives blighted by sin, inescapably answerable to the sin-hating God.[5]

Here's how Moses put it:

> For we have been consumed by Your anger
> And by Your wrath we have been dismayed.
> You have placed our iniquities before You,
> Our secret sins in the light of Your presence.
> For all our days have declined in Your fury;
> We have finished our years like a sigh. (vv. 7–9)

Our sins, and Adam and Eve's original sin, mark every facet of our lives. The fact that we quickly age and inevitably die point to sin's effects. The fact that we need a Savior who will take God's wrath for us points to what our sin has done. And sometimes when we're stuck in monotony's stagnating sameness, not eagerly participating in life the way God meant us to, we can't help but think that our sins may have led us there as well.

My Days Are So Empty

Shadowing Moses' reflection on God's anger is a sense of emptiness.

> As for the days of our life, they contain seventy years,
> Or if due to strength, eighty years,
> Yet their pride is but labor and sorrow;

5. J. A. Motyer, "The Psalms," in the *New Bible Commentary: 21st Century Edition*, 4th ed., revised (Downers Grove, Ill.: InterVarsity Press, 1994), p. 545.

For soon it is gone and we fly away.
Who understands the power of Your anger
And Your fury, according to the fear that is due You?
(vv. 10–11)

What is the answer to the futility and sadness sin has created? Moses gives us the answer in the last verses of his psalm.

Bringing the Song

As Moses ends his psalm, he asks for the Lord's presence and blessing in a series of requests.

> So teach us to number our days,
> That we may present to You a heart of wisdom.
> Do return, O Lord; how long will it be?
> And be sorry for Your servants.
> O satisfy us in the morning with Your lovingkindness,
> That we may sing for joy and be glad all our days.
> Make us glad according to the days You have
>   afflicted us,
> And the years we have seen evil.
> Let Your work appear to Your servants
> And Your majesty to their children.
> Let the favor of the Lord our God be upon us;
> And confirm for us the work of our hands;
> Yes, confirm the work of our hands. (vv. 12–17)

J. A. Motyer brings out the rich meaning in Moses' requests as well as the remedy for our sin-caused sorrow.

> It is by prayer that we counter the disintegrative power of sin, by prayer that we fly to the God whom we have offended, by prayer that we take up our *dwelling place* (1) in him. This was the way of Moses. . . . To preserve [ourselves] there are four aspects of prayer: recognize our limited time so as to use it with wisdom (12); cry for compassion from a reconciled God (13); counter the withering of life (the *morning* of 5–6) with a new *morning* filled with his *love* which does not change *all our days* (14); look to him to make life as full of gladness as otherwise it would have been of affliction (15). Here are

the four strong walls of our eternal dwelling in God: he is our wisdom (12, 1 Cor. 1:30), our forgiveness (13, Is. 55:7), our stability throughout our days (14, 73:26), our renewal (15, Rom. 6:4–8).[6]

God also gives value to our work—the work we do for and in Him (Ps. 90:17). He, the Eternal One, remembers what we do (see 1 Cor. 15:58; Heb. 6:10), giving it a permanence that this world can never match.

So when we look to the Lord, ponder His eternal existence, make our home in Him, and seek our satisfaction in Him, the gray meaninglessness of monotony will fade away to reveal true life in all its vibrant color. Come to Him, won't you, and let Him transform the empty drone of boredom into a song of joy (Ps. 90:14)!

Living Insights

G. K. Chesterton gives us this insight: "There is no such thing on earth as an uninteresting subject; the only thing that can exist is an uninterested person."[7]

Do you agree? When your life feels monotonous, do you tend to focus on your circumstances or look for causes within yourself?

_____

_____

_____

_____

_____

6. Motyer, "The Psalms," in *The New Bible Commentary,* p. 545.

7. G. K. Chesterton, as quoted in Microsoft Bookshelf 98, copyright © and ℗ 1987–1996 Microsoft Corporation. All rights reserved. From *The Columbia Dictionary of Quotations,* licensed from Columbia University Press. Copyright © 1995 by Columbia University Press. All rights reserved.

Certain activities and situations can leave us feeling empty, there's no doubt about that. What seems to drain the color out of your life?

_____

_____

_____

_____

_____

If everything in your outer world is fine, what may be happening inside of you that is making life feel meaningless? Are you feeling disconnected somehow? Depressed? Weary? What has taken the purpose out of what you do?

_____

_____

_____

_____

_____

Reread and reflect on Moses' psalm. What gives you the most hope—what lifts your spirit and reinstates your sense of purpose?

_____

_____

_____

_____

_____

As frail and transitory as we are, God still delights for us to share in His work (see Eph. 2:10). May His grace dispel our apathy and help us realize that each day counts for Him!

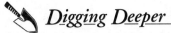 *Digging Deeper*

Does the thought of God's wrath ever trouble you? Do you ever feel that it's not fair? Ray Stedman grappled with these questions and came to a conclusion that should set your mind at ease.

> Surely this phrase, "the wrath of God," is greatly misunderstood by many people. Many think invariably of some sort of peeved deity, a kind of cosmic, terrible-tempered Mr. Bang, who indulges in violent and uncontrolled displays of temper when we human beings do not do what we ought to do. But such a concept only reveals the limitations of our understanding. The Bible never deals with the wrath of God that way.
>
> According to the Scriptures, the wrath of God is God's moral integrity. When a man refuses to yield himself to God, he creates certain conditions (not only for himself but for others as well), which God has ordained for harm. It is God who makes evil result in sorrow, heartache, injustice and despair. It is God' way of saying to man, "Look, you must face the truth. You were made for me. If you, in the dignity of human choice that I have given you, decide that you don't want me, then I will leave. But you will have to bear the consequences." The absence of God is destructive to human life. That absence is God's wrath and God cannot withhold it. In His moral integrity God insists that evil things should occur as a result of man's choice. . . . The cause of God's wrath then is always human sin.[8]

---

8. Ray C. Stedman, *Psalms of Faith* (Ventura, Calif.: Gospel Light Publications, Regal Books, 1988), pp. 243–44.

Chapter 8

GROWING THROUGH FEAR

Psalm 27

*P*sssst. Can I tell you a secret? Just between us? I have a . . . er . . . a condition. It's called *ophidiophobia*. Oh, don't worry—it's not contagious! (At least I don't think it is.) And it doesn't really hurt—except when I'm out on a beautiful mountain trail. Then it can make my heart pound, my palms sweat, and my legs go wobbly.

You see, *ophidiophobia* is the scientific name for the fear of snakes.

And, at least for me, they don't have to be real snakes, either. Just turning the page of a magazine or newspaper and unexpectedly finding the picture of a snake is enough to shoot the old adrenaline sky-high.

Do you have any fears like this? Come on now, be honest—everyone is afraid of something. On the Internet, the Phobia List, a whole site dedicated to providing an alphabetical listing of phobias, names 524 of them! Clearly, fear is a tightly woven thread in the fabric of the human psyche.

Not all fears, of course, are phobias. However, phobias and garden-variety fears generally have one trait in common: they limit our involvement in life. Fear makes our world smaller. When it attacks, we tend to pull back, to retreat. Rather than meet what we are afraid of head-on, we hide at home or sleep or overeat or make excuses. And the boundaries of our world shrink bit by frightened bit.

Quiet mountain trails become gauntlets of treacherous viper pits to me, so I don't often go hiking. But because I succumb to this fear, I also forfeit the beauty and peace that nature offers to a city-weary soul.

What do you fear—and forfeit?

Maybe you're afraid to admit you are afraid. Afraid that you are the only one—the only child of God—who struggles with fear. Everyone else, at least from your point of view, seems so strong, so sure. But this is a mistaken idea, as Dr. Paul Tournier explains:

> There are not, . . . as is commonly believed, two kinds of human beings, those who have inner conflicts and those who do not. If there is a distinction to be made among men, it is rather this: some hide their fears, while others admit them. Nevertheless,

to recognize our fears and look them in the face, is frightening; but it is the only way of holding our own against them.[1]

Would you like to hold your own against your fears—push out the boundaries of your world even a little bit? Then let's turn to Psalm 27, where we'll learn from David how we can overcome our fears and who is our source of confidence.

An Overall Glance

David is so human—and so real. He doesn't spiritualize his fears or try to pretend them away. Even an overall glance at the scope and structure of this psalm reveals his honesty.

Scope

Psalm 27 can be divided easily into two distinct sections. In verses 1–6, David exudes a confidence that comes from keeping his faith trained on God. Then, in the latter half, his mood shifts and his confident affirmations turn to a desperate, yearning prayer.

Because of the dissimilar tone of these sections, some scholars believe that they are actually two different psalms edited together. Commentator James Montgomery Boice, however, sees an essential unity.

> What we have here is an unfolding of two closely related moods by the same inspired author, put together like two movements of a symphony. And the point is that these two apparently opposing moods are also often in us, frequently at the same time or at nearly the same time. Don't you find that you are often both confident and anxious, trusting and fearful, or at least that your mood swings easily from one to the other? I do. It is part of what it means to be a weak human being.[2]

1. Paul Tournier, *The Strong and the Weak*, trans. Edwin Hudson (Philadelphia, Pa.: Westminster Press, 1963), p. 91.

2. James Montgomery Boice, *Psalms, Volume 1: Psalms 1–41* (Grand Rapids, Mich.: Baker Books, 1994), p. 238.

Structure

One way to outline David's psalm is like this:

- Verse 1: Theme—"The Lord is my light and my salvation; Whom shall I fear?"
- Verses 2–6: Declaration of Trust
- Verses 7–13: Prayer for Support
- Verse 14: Encouragement to Wait on the Lord

Notice the progression David makes. He begins by affirming his confidence that the Lord will keep him safe. Then his joy ebbs, yet he steadfastly seeks the Lord through his fear. Finally, having held onto his confidence, he comes through his fear and encourages us to place our confidence in the Lord as well.

Even at a glance, David's psalm encourages us with its honesty and hopeful outcome. Let's draw even closer now to partake of his confidence in the steadfast and ever-loving Lord and make David's words of faith in the midst of fear our own.

An Internal Analysis

David's first words of bold trust in the Lord give us the theme of his psalm.

Theme

> The Lord is my light and my salvation;
> Whom shall I fear?
> The Lord is the defense of my life;
> Whom shall I dread? (Ps. 27:1)

The Lord does not just provide but *is* David's "light," "salvation," and "defense."[3] Over in the New Testament, John tells us that "God is Light, and in Him there is no darkness at all" (1 John 1:5). God is pure light—righteous and holy. He guides and directs us, enlightening our minds with understanding. We grow and have life in His light, much like nature flourishes in the sunlight. And remember, the first thing God created was light (Gen. 1:3), and He still dispels darkness and all its fearsome shadows today.

---

3. Other Old Testament passages use light to describe God, but only in Psalm 27 is He called "light." Darkness cannot triumph over the all-powerful God who is light.

That's why He is also our "salvation" or deliverance—we are rescued from darkness to be brought into the safety of His light. This reassuring truth pertains not only to earthly enemies, as was probably David's case, but also to spiritual assailants, as Paul relates.

> "The Lord said, . . . '[I] appoint you a minister . . . to open their eyes so that they may turn from darkness to light and from the dominion of Satan to God, that they may receive forgiveness of sins and an inheritance among those who have been sanctified by faith in Me.'" (Acts 26:15–18)

God is also our "defense" or stronghold, a refuge from attacks and danger. He is our protection against the enemy of our souls, our safe place in an often unsafe world.

No wonder, then, that David can say, "Whom shall I fear? . . . Whom shall I dread?" (Ps. 27:1). With the Creator and Sustainer of the universe watching over him, David could rest confidently in the Lord rather than tremble with anxiety and intimidation. It was God's strength, not his own, that would see him through.

Declaration of Trust

David certainly had plenty to tremble about. As Charles Spurgeon notes, "The enemies of our souls are not deficient in ferocity. . . . Like cannibals they would make a full end of the man, tear him limb from limb, and make a feast for their malice."[4] But because of God's strength, David did not fear nor dread even a host of rapacious enemies.

> When evildoers came upon me to devour my flesh,
> My adversaries and my enemies, they stumbled
> and fell.
> Though a host encamp against me,
> My heart will not fear;
> Though war arise against me,
> In spite of this I shall be confident. (vv. 2–3)

With hostile forces all around him, how could David keep his

---

4. C. H. Spurgeon, *The Treasury of David*, vol. 1, Psalm 1 to 57 (McLean, Va.: MacDonald Publishing Co., n.d.), part 2, p. 2.

heart from faltering with fear? By taking sanctuary in the Lord.

> One thing I have asked from the Lord, that I shall seek:
> That I may dwell in the house of the Lord all the
> days of my life,
> To behold the beauty of the Lord
> And to meditate in His temple.
> For in the day of trouble He will conceal me in His
> tabernacle;
> In the secret place of His tent He will hide me;
> He will lift me up on a rock.
> And now my head will be lifted up above my
> enemies around me,
> And I will offer in His tent sacrifices with shouts of joy;
> I will sing, yes, I will sing praises to the Lord.
> (vv. 4–6)

Invariably, when we are intimidated, we are more conscious of the cause of our fear than we are of our Lord. David, however, sought *one thing:* spiritual intimacy with God. He wanted to live in close communion with the Lord, linger on His beauty, and seek His presence. With the infinite goodness of God filling his perspective, David's fears faded. He knew he could shelter his heart and mind within the walls of God's strength and stand secure on the rock of God's assurance. What joy he took in God's care of him! His heart swelled with praise, and he wanted nothing more than to sing to God at the top of his lungs.

If only David's psalm ended here. Wouldn't it be nice to have our fears replaced with joy, to have our focus so set on the Lord that nothing could shake us? Unfortunately, life isn't like that, and David comes down from the mountaintop of praise to the valley of desperate prayer—just like we all do.[5]

Prayer for Support

Fear wasn't done with David yet. But even when he felt small

---

5. Dr. Tournier writes, "What also humiliates and torments many people is the discovery of the inconstancy of their feelings. They tell us: 'I envy you your assured and constant faith; I am always going up and down between the heights and the depths!' Truly, we are all like that, for the motions of the mind and heart are indeed movements. If there were no movement, we should perceive nothing. Faith itself is a perpetual and determined return towards God, from whom we are constantly turning away." *The Strong and the Weak,* p. 85.

and weak, he still clung to the Lord.

> Hear, O Lord, when I cry with my voice,
> And be gracious to me and answer me.
> When You said, "Seek My face," my heart said to You,
> "Your face, O Lord, I shall seek."
> Do not hide Your face from me,
> Do not turn Your servant away in anger;
> You have been my help;
> Do not abandon me nor forsake me,
> O God of my salvation!
> For my father and my mother have forsaken me,[6]
> But the Lord will take me up. (vv. 7–10)

This is no half-hearted petition! David's words possess a boldness and fervency of one not afraid of trusting absolutely in God (see also Heb. 4:16). In fact, his confidence most likely arose from "a period of searching and doubt, out of which true faith develops and leads to a more determined reliance on God."[7]

And David relied on the Lord, turning to Him for guidance and relief.

> Teach me Your way, O Lord,
> And lead me in a level path
> Because of my foes.
> Do not deliver me over to the desire of my adversaries,
> For false witnesses have risen against me,
> And such as breathe out violence.
> I would have despaired unless I had believed that I
>   would see the goodness of the Lord
> In the land of the living. (Ps. 27:11–13)

Encouragement to Wait on the Lord

The last verse of David's psalm brings us full circle to where we began our study of growing pains—to waiting. But rather than

---

6. According to the NASB margin note, this verse can also be rendered: "If my father and my mother forsake me, Then the Lord will take me up." Meaning more figuratively that "even if the strongest human love should reach its limit, the Lord's love remains." J. A. Motyer, "The Psalms," in the *New Bible Commentary: 21st Century Edition*, 4th ed., rev. (Downers Grove, Ill.: InterVarsity Press, 1994), p. 503.

7. Willem A. VanGemeren, "Psalms," in *The Expositor's Bible Commentary*, gen. ed. Frank E. Gaebelein (Grand Rapids, Mich.: Zondervan Publishing House, 1991), vol. 5, p. 246.

waiting in frustration, David urges us to wait expectantly, in eagerness, in confidence.

> Wait for the Lord;
> Be strong and let your heart take courage;
> Yes, wait for the Lord. (v. 14)

God is our light, salvation, and stronghold, remember (v. 1)? He is good and the Giver of good things. So when your fears mount, take your eyes off of them and look to the Lord—don't retreat and let fear shrink your world, but lean into God and let Him take you through your fear and beyond. He can do it, and He waits to help you do it too.

🌸 Living Insights

One of our greatest struggles with fear is admitting that we are afraid. "We always want to seem strong," Dr. Paul Tournier observes. "We are ashamed of our fear, and this shame consolidates the fear and renders it harmful."[8]

The solution? Honesty. Not worrying about how we look to others, but just being real—which, being human, means being weak sometimes. OK, a lot of the time. Just think, if everyone was honest about being fearful and weak, nobody would be worried about always having to look strong. Wouldn't that be a relief? So being honest is the first step. The next is to bring our fears to God, as Dr. Tournier explains.

> A woman patient of mine, suffering from a tumour in the breast, writes to me about her fear of cancer: "A real Christian ought not to be afraid." No, madam, the Christian is not exempt from fear, but he takes his fears to God. Faith does not suppress fear; what it does is to allow one to go forward in spite of it. When my English friend made his list of fears it was so as to face them—with God's grace. In God's presence we abandon the stoic's utopia of a life without fear, which is the source of so many repressions and so many lies.

8. Tournier, *The Strong and the Weak*, p. 93.

. . . Grace is promised to him who recognizes his weakness, and not to him who boasts of his strength. The Bible, with its realistic knowledge of the human heart, repeats 365 times the words "Fear not." It speaks also of "the fear of God" as the beginning of wisdom. Christ, with his psychological insight, knows that there is no life without fear.[9]

What fears do you struggle with? Have you ever admitted them to anyone? If you haven't, how about starting by admitting them to yourself on paper?

_____

_____

_____

What have your fears made you forfeit? How have they made your life smaller?

_____

_____

_____

Which areas currently hemmed in by fear would you most like to expand? What would your life look like if you let God bring you beyond these fears?

_____

_____

_____

Fear will always be a part of our lives. But so will God's grace. Take your fears to Him, won't you? He'll help you, as He did David, to go forward and have fullness of life in spite of your fears.

9. Tournier, The Strong and the Weak, p. 93.

BOOKS FOR
PROBING FURTHER

Most of us wouldn't mind learning about growing pains in an air-conditioned classroom with a silver-tongued professor from an easy-to-read book. We could even handle tests—as long as they weren't pop quizzes—and we'd endure a light amount of homework.

But then there's real life . . .

The courses on waiting, failure, misunderstanding, loss, mistakes, weakness, monotony, and fear often come when we least expect or want them. And we usually don't learn their lessons in a comfortable, orderly fashion either. Like the psalmist, sometimes the best we can do is cry out to God,

> Turn to me and be gracious to me
> for I am lonely and afflicted.
> The troubles of my heart have multiplied.
> (Ps. 25:16–17a NIV)

Hopefully, along with the practical insights you've gained from this study, you've also learned how near God is to you, how much He cares, and how strong and reliable He is. Hopefully, you've begun to learn how to turn to Him the way David did.

> Make me know Your ways, O Lord;
> Teach me Your paths.
> Lead me in Your truth and teach me,
> For You are the God of my salvation;
> For You I wait all the day.
> Remember, O Lord, Your compassion and Your
>   lovingkindnesses,
> For they have been from of old. . . .
> According to Your lovingkindness remember me,
> For Your goodness' sake, O Lord. (vv. 4–7)

If you would like to learn more about growing closer to the Lord through the Psalms and growing deeper as His child through your pain, the following resources will help you. God bless!

The Psalms

Boice, James Montgomery. *Psalms, Volume 1: Psalms 1–41*. Grand Rapids, Mich.: Baker Books, 1994.

———. *Psalms, Volume 2: Psalms 42–106*. Grand Rapids, Mich.: Baker Books, 1996.

———. *Psalms, Volume 3: Psalms 107–150*. Grand Rapids, Mich.: Baker Books, 1998.

Brueggemann, Walter. *Praying the Psalms*. Winona, Minn.: Saint Mary's Press, 1993.

Fee, Gordon D., and Douglas Stuart. *How to Read the Bible for All Its Worth*. Grand Rapids, Mich.: Zondervan Publishing House, Academie Books, 1982.

Peterson, Eugene H. *Answering God: The Psalms as Tools for Prayer*. San Francisco, Calif.: HarperSanFrancisco, 1989.

The Pains

Berkley, James D. *Making the Most of Mistakes*. Leadership Library, vol. 11. Dallas, Tex.: Word Books, 1987.

Counseling Insights: A Biblical Perspective on Caring for People. From the Counseling ministry of Insight for Living. 2 volumes. Anaheim, Calif.: Insight for Living, 1997, 1998, 1999.

Kreeft, Peter. *Making Sense Out of Suffering*. Ann Arbor, Mich.: Servant Books, 1986.

Kübler-Ross, Elisabeth. *On Death and Dying*. New York, N.Y.: Macmillan Publishing Co., 1969.

Lutzer, Erwin W. *Failure: The Back Door to Success*. Chicago, Ill.: Moody Press, 1975.

Patterson, Ben. *Waiting: Finding Hope When God Seems Silent*. Downers Grove, Ill.: InterVarsity Press, 1989.

Tournier, Paul. *The Strong and the Weak*. Translated by Edwin Hudson. Philadelphia, Pa.: Westminster Press, 1963.

Yancey, Philip. *Disappointment with God*. Grand Rapids, Mich.: Zondervan Publishing House, 1988.

Some of these books may be out of print and available only through a library. For those currently available, please contact your local Christian bookstore. Books by Charles R. Swindoll, as well as some books by other authors, may be obtained through Insight for Living.

Insight for Living also offers study guides on many books of the Bible, as well as on a variety of issues and Bible characters. For more information, see the ordering instructions that follow and contact the office that serves you.

NOTES

_____

_____

_____

_____

_____

_____

_____

_____

_____

_____

_____

_____

_____

NOTES

NOTES

NOTES

ORDERING INFORMATION

GROWING PAINS

If you would like to order additional study guides, purchase the cassette series that accompanies this guide, or request our product catalogs, please contact the office that serves you.

United States and International locations:

Insight for Living
Post Office Box 69000
Anaheim, CA 92817-0900

1-800-772-8888, 24 hours a day, 7 days a week
(714) 575-5000, 8:00 A.M. to 4:30 P.M., Pacific time, Monday to Friday

Canada:

Insight for Living Ministries
Post Office Box 2510
Vancouver, BC, Canada V6B 3W7

1-800-663-7639, 24 hours a day, 7 days a week

Australia:

Insight for Living, Inc.
General Post Office Box 2823 EE
Melbourne, VIC 3001, Australia

Toll-free 1800-772-888 or (03) 9877-4277, 8:30 A.M. to 5:00 P.M., Monday to Friday

World Wide Web:
www.insight.org

Study Guide Subscription Program

Study guide subscriptions are available. Please call or write the office nearest you to find out how you can receive our study guides on a regular basis.